SONS OF ALBION

THE INSIDE STORY OF THE SECTION 5 SQUAD INCORPORATING THE CLUBHOUSE AND SMETHWICK MOB, 30+ YEARS OF WEST BROM'S HOOLIGAN FIRMS

By Tony Freeth, Snarka and Big Jon

Order this book online at www.trafford.com
or email orders@trafford.com

Most Trafford titles are also available at major online book retailers.

Note for Librarians: A cataloguing record for this book is available from Library
and Archives Canada at www.collectionscanada.ca/amicus/index-e.html

Printed in Victoria, BC, Canada.

ISBN: 978-1-4251-8855-9

*Our mission is to efficiently provide the world's finest, most comprehensive
book publishing service, enabling every author to experience success.
To find out how to publish your book, your way, and have it available
worldwide, visit us online at www.trafford.com*

Trafford rev. 9/15/2009

www.trafford.com

North America & international
toll-free: 1 888 232 4444 (USA & Canada)
phone: 250 383 6864 ♦ fax: 812 355 4082

Tony: Dedicated to my mum Evelyn Freeth (RIP), and to all my family. Special thanks must go to my in-laws John and Sylvia Stanier who treat me as their own and never stop believing in me.

Snarka: To my nan, Violet, and my dad, Joe, (RIP), mom June, and all my family and friends.

Jon: To all my family who have stood by me through thick and thin and to all Albion lads, past and present. It's our turn to set the record straight.

Contents

Introduction

Snarka: I first thought about doing a book a few years ago as a lot of Albion's older faces and quite a few younger ones were saying I should write about the Clubhouse days in the early-Eighties. I'd started to read a few of the so-called hooligan books and thought why not?

I never really thought of myself as one, I just love my football and the Albion in particular and I was lucky enough to be around at the time of the emergence of football Casuals. I did get involved in my fair share of battles at matches, as did a large percentage of people, so I thought I'd give it ago but, it turned to out to be nigh on impossible. I have a terrible memory for dates and places - not good when trying to tell stories from 20-plus years ago - and lads who said they would give me their side of stories never did. So, really, that's as far as I got until I got talking to Tony Freeth at a match – he'll probably know the time, date what we were wearing with his great memory. He said he was also trying to write a book about his era, the Section 5 Squad, who were Albion's main firm after the Clubhouse days had come to an end. We decided to pool our stories and write a book together.

That all went along fine until we reached a point where we didn't really know how to get it on the shelves. Tony had been in contact with a well-known football author but had been let down at the last minute. So we were stuck. We mentioned this to Big Jon who knew some of the lads who were involved with the Zulus book. He then got in touch with Caroline Gall the author and also author of the Leeds Service Crew book and she agreed to take it on for us. Me and Tony also asked Jon if he wanted to come on board which he agreed to.

So, we now had three of us doing the book and things went quickly then as Jon as worked tirelessly on fundraising and getting stories in. I wanted to tell my story as I think so-called Soccer Casuals are an important part of British youth culture, dismissed by society as just hooligans. To me it's the only culture that's not music related. Its clothes, football and more importantly respect from mates and other Casuals and I was at the forefront of that movement in West Brom from the early-Eighties.

I've tried to be as honest as I can but obviously some will disagree with my accounts of events and others may wonder why their teams' stories are not included.

But let's be honest, most teams don't want to be remembered by the bad times and as it's about our team, most of our successes will be mentioned before our failures.

I would like to thank first and foremost Tony and Jon for all the work they've done, Caroline Gall for all her input at meetings and my wife, Lynne, for putting up with the meetings and hours of typing.

My old Clubhouse mates, Sooty, Wozza, Malek and Twinny and Budgie, the Old Smethwick mob top face, who never did get his stories to me. Thanks to John Connally, Bowie, Mutley, Pona, Basher, Seery, Frankie, Paynee, Tucker, Eamon and Gav Moore (RIP), all top boys in their day and to JL, Albion's top boy for 20-plus years - good luck and all the best for the future from my family to yours.

Also, my daughter, Taylor, and step-kids Steph and Matt, Nelson, my Staffie, and of course my daft cousin Netty, a true legend at the Albion - just a pity she was born a girl.

And finally, to my mom and dad (RIP) who gave me the greatest gift of all, my love of the ALBION.

Tony: I originally had the idea for this book about three years ago and after a few half-hearted attempts with Cola, a lad involved with West Brom since the mid-Eighties, I seemed to give up. It was then I got in touch with Snarka, someone I had a very healthy respect for over the years but we couldn't sort out how to get it from written memoirs to an actual book, cue Big Jon's input. He had been involved since the mid-Nineties and was the sort of lad who would put his heart and soul into things and after careful deliberation, me and Snarka invited him on-board. This is where things started to take off as within weeks, Jon contacted Caroline Gall.

Our subsequent meeting went well and I was surprised how enthusiastic Caroline was but, bad news came a few weeks later. Milo Books weren't interested in doing any more football violence books – so what now? Caroline and Jon got in contact with Trafford Publishing, a self-publication outfit and we were up and running again.

Countless meetings and hours locked away writing, phoning around and organising photo-shoots followed. At times I felt, is it worth it? But yes, putting the record straight is. This book is NOT to gain any sort of notoriety for the authors. It's for everyone. Don't be upset if your name isn't mentioned, maybe we don't know it or maybe we didn't know if certain lads wanted their names in a book connecting them to football violence. But none-the-less, this book is for every Albion lad, not just us three.

A very special thank you should come from all of us to Caroline as I'm certain our book would never have made it onto the shelves if not for her kindness and dedication throughout the whole affair. I just hope you will all be as proud of it as we are.

Respect and regards
Tony Freeth

Jon: I first considered doing a book on my own whilst in prison, probably mainly down to boredom more than anything else. After thinking long and hard about it, my feelings were that really I didn't have the memory or material to fill one. After my release, I considered approaching several lads about doing a book but I never got around to doing anything about it. Some time later and by sheer coincidence, Tony approached me to ask me to write about some incidents we were both involved in which then led to him asking me to join him and Snarka as a joint author.

If I do anything, I do it properly. I am a very good organiser and I do have contacts country-wide who have enabled us to get the book together and they've also helped with a whole host of things with the book. I got in touch with Caroline through a Blues contact and she was highly recommended, and ever since she first came on board she's been golden.

I feel the book is a long-time coming. We needed to have our say and the lads involved have all played a major part over the years with Tony, Snarka and others like Bowie and Peachy being prime examples of that. I don't consider that I've done anything of great note. I've been involved in more than my fair share of chaos and from the mid-Nineties up until 2004, I was heavily involved in organising a lot of what our firm did. I think that during that period our firm was organised and more than decent.

We did not travel en masse that often but for big games - local derbies in particular - we were always organised and on the ball. More importantly, we made every effort to front our rivals rather than making life easy with police escorts.

Sometimes our planning involved military precision and more often than not it worked and our not-so intelligence police were left chasing shadows.

I'm now on a banning order but can sit back safe in the knowledge that on our day, we are a force to be reckoned with and in our local area we have done more than the vast majority of firms put together. The only regret from this book is that more of the main faces did not get involved. We have to respect their wishes and after all, we know what has occurred over the years and who has done what so that's all that matters.

Everyone in the firm is fully aware of who our main face is, he needs no introduction and it's a shame he couldn't be more involved. He is a main man in every sense of the word. What he says, he does without question. His status is legendary.

This book is only a part of what has occurred but it is a very good representation of West Brom's lads and that, in my eyes, is good enough. Hopefully in the future an updated version will be released and all will be revealed. I certainly hope so.

PART ONE

Chapter One

Stoking up the Fire

Tony: I was born on the 17 February 1965 at Avonside Hospital in Evesham, Worcester. I was the illegitimate child of a 17-year-old single girl, who, with no husband and her father ashamed and distraught, insisted I was put up for adoption. So, on 14 April of the same year I was adopted at a kid's home in Malvern. The couple that arrived that day were none other than Eric and Evelyn Freeth, who had lost twins earlier in their marriage. They had been told that they would never have kids of their own and apparently my mom-to-be took one look at me, and well, moms being moms, loved me instantly. I wonder how many times in life she regretted that decision? But, knowing my mom, never, no matter what. Yes, it was a very happy pair who took their first son back to their council flat in Oldbury, on the outskirts of West Bromwich. I was indeed the lucky one as I had inherited two wonderful parents.

You see, I didn't come from a broken home or, one with continual arguments or domestic violence. Our home was full of love and laughter and for all my wrong- doings later on in life, my mother worshipped me always. My father was a toolsetter and worked hard for a small wage. They then had two lads of their own - good old NHS advice ay? With the arrival of Brian and Gary, it must have stretched the finances considerably and we were probably one of the poorest families on the estate.

Our estate was rough, not as rough as others in the borough but, none-the-less fighting was definitely part of everyday life in Lodge Street, Oldbury. Lovely grey concrete maisonettes lined our estate, which brought every race, creed and colour to it. As on any estate, there were the usual bully boys, who I took a lot of slaps from in my early days, but you learn to cope with it. My schooling began at Christchurch C of E (infants). I can't remember too much to be honest but I do remember a lot more of my primary school, St Francis Xavier in McKean Road. I learnt how to box there - which would come in handy with the bullies later - and like most boys fell in love with football.

I lived, ate and breathed it and my wife will tell you I still do. Like most boys, I dreamed of becoming a footballer. I captained the school team on a number of occasions, but like most, didn't develop into anything that special. So it was around this time in my life I started to go up the Albion, as did most lads on the estate. Me and my best mate, Daz Guy, used to go to most of the home games and a little later on in life went to the away games as well. We were totally obsessed with West Brom and at these times we had the likes of Cyrille Regis, Laurie Cunningham, Tony Brown and others playing in a very good Albion team. Many Saturdays we'd try to sneak through adults' legs or get up there really early and climb over the walls into the outside toilets at the Smethwick End of the ground.

Some weekends, to try and get the money together to go up the game, me Daz, and his older brother, Dean, would go around to peoples' homes and ask if they had anything they didn't want, anything from a plant to a settee. We'd then cart it up to Oldbury High Street to a little second-hand shop to get the money for the match. The old man there, George, must have dreaded Saturdays, but we were so determined. I think he gave us the money because he felt sorry for us but we would do just about anything to get up the Hawthorns.

Like most kids that grew up on council estates, we were little urchins always up to mischief and always getting bollocked by the neighbours. But, all in I would say we were lovable rogues. By this time, I was attending Albright High School in Oldbury and was at the stage in my life when you start looking up to people. Unfortunately for me – and probably my parents - it seemed to be football hooligans.

I'll always remember in Art, my form tutor, Mr Dawson, a smashing bloke, standing over my shoulder as I drew. He stopped me, picked up the piece of paper and shook his head and asked me: "Why are you drawing a picture of bootboys wearing football scarves and fighting?" "I don't know sir" was my pathetic reply. "Tony" he said. "Why do you look up to these people? You will never get anywhere in life following people like that." At the time, I thought: "Bollocks". But I would never dare say that to him. He was a big, old rugby player and had quite a temper when he lost it, but none the less a really good man to me and I really did like him. Even though I was the first pupil he ever caned.

Back up the Baggies, and this was the Smethwick mob days up the Hawthorns, Daz and I would follow all the heads around and watch them in action - legends like Bowie, Rogers, Seery, Budgie. Proper game lads. We were all addicted to it, although still too young to get involved but it would only be a matter of time. We'd play at it over and over again re-enacting some of the violent clashes we'd witnessed. Then, in the late Seventies, as the skinhead culture kicked in, we again followed. I remember there being loads of skins up the Albion, as there was at most clubs at the time. I particularly got very involved in the whole skinhead movement and started to drift away from Oldbury and West Bromwich and moved over to Cradley Heath where we had built up quite a formidable crew of skinheads. We'd bash just about anyone who tried it on with us at the time. I, like many of the others, were having trouble kicking glue sniffing. Yeah, I know it sounds twattish now, but back in the day it was a real epidemic. We really used to get fucked-up on the stuff, which obviously led to a lot of trouble as a young boy.

The little things about drawing fans fighting etc, I, like many others, indulged in such fantasies but this book is for us West Brom firms to give our side of the coin, not for me to gain any sort of recognition as a "top lad". In fact, similar to what Jasper says in his book – Naughty - about the Stoke lads, there wasn't really a "top lad". There was, as in every firm, a main bunch of us who seemed to be first in most times. But, a leader? Some, like me, had bigger mouths. Ha ha.

* * * * * * *

My first experience of football violence was at the last home game of the 1977 season. I remember a gap opening up on the Brummie Road end and the cry went up of "City, City!"

A deafening roar was heard as the swaying, baying crowd surged forward and attacked. Fists and boots were flying with people running in all directions and always that deafening roar. I was filled with a feeling of both fear and excitement as my pals and I ran for cover. Around 30 Stoke City fans had infiltrated the end traditionally occupied by the home support of West Brom. The fighting seemed to last for ages but, in truth was probably a couple of minutes before the police led the proud but battered and bruised mob around the side of the pitch to a heroes welcome from the large travelling support who occupied the Smethwick End.

As me and my young mates stood in our original places, yet another roar and a gap appeared only this time the gap was amongst the Stoke support. Albion's bootboys, as they were probably known back then, about 30-strong, obviously had the same idea. We had a great view of the heaving masses at the other end. It seemed like a more violent encounter than the previous one by Stoke but eventually the police got to grips with them and led our heroes back to our end of the ground. As the gates were unlocked to let them in, I couldn't help but feel proud of them.

There were six young friends together that day as Albion beat Stoke 3-0 and, for two of us, it was to have a lasting effect on the way we perceived what following a football team was all about. To say I hadn't been scared out of my wits would have been a total untruth, but the fact was, I became infatuated by what some would call the misguided loyalty of the football "hooligans". In the years that followed, me and my best mate Daz Guy would follow the ever growing movement of Albion's bootboys and especially the Smethwick End mob later on. We were always at a safe distance but always close enough to see every charge, punch, kick or headbutt. We were absolutely obsessed with it all. As I have already said, back on our lovely council estate by Oldbury town centre about a mile from West Bromwich, often the game of the day would be football violence, with lads splitting into two gangs to fight. We lived and breathed West Brom and the violent fan culture surrounding it. As the years rolled by Daz and I got heavily involved in the skinhead culture, as did so many other fans up and down the country. We witnessed many violent exchanges between rival shaven-headed fans.

As so often happens in life, friends for one reason or another drift apart and I moved out of Oldbury and saw less and less of my boyhood pals and didn't frequent the Hawthorns very often for the next couple of seasons. Then on my 19th birthday in 1984 I decided to go up. We'd drawn Plymouth Argyle in the FA Cup and I just had a good feeling about it. This match, unbeknown to me at the time, really did change my life for the next 20 years or so. As I ordered myself a pint in the Sandwell pub on West Bromwich High Street, I became aware that I was sticking out like a sore thumb as all the unfamiliar faces were dressed in the new uniform of the football thug - Fila, Tacchini, Lacoste,

Burberry. It was everywhere I looked, things really had changed. I felt a bit uneasy, but then caught sight of my old mate Daz who greeted me with much enthusiasm before filling me in on what the score was now up the Albion. It was apparent that a new mob or "firm" as every football gang was calling itself now, had evolved under the name the Clubhouse and was led by a lad called Snarka. The firm had infiltrated many home ends on its travels and was apparently getting quite a name for itself. I scanned the pub and started to recognise many faces from the skinhead era. Obviously these lads had become "trendy" and grown their hair. As kick off approached, the large mob made the long walk to the ground. I wasn't aware of any aggro on the way, but I was aware of the change in peoples' behaviour - the walk, the talk, everything and everyone had changed. But, the continual question of: "Where's your boys?" was asked to certain away followers.

To be honest, at the time I didn't feel part of what was going on, it all seemed very alien to me. We lost the game 1-0 and it was awful. Towards the end, Daz came over to me and said there would be a meeting of all our boys at the back of the Smethwick End. I just had to see for myself what exactly was going on. I could see maybe up to a couple of hundred or so lads, hanging around the top of the ramp that led down to behind the away pen. As the final whistle went everyone made their way onto Halfords Lane at the same time as the Plymouth fans came pouring out celebrating a famous victory. It ended up a total free-for-all as the unsuspecting Argyle firm got battered from pillar to post. Anyone game enough got it. I found myself punching my way through them, it was total mayhem. The police eventually regained control with Albion's firm baton-charged over to the other side of the road.

I could hear someone shouting "Skin! Skin!" over and over again. I could see it was a tall, rough looking lad who was beckoning for me to join them. As I approached him he said "Fair-play Skin". I didn't know it at the time, but the lad's name was Johnny Payne, and over the next few years he was to become a trusted friend of mine as well as becoming probably the first ever "top boy" in the Section 5 Squad, which came together later in the mid-Eighties. John was sound and game as fuck. He is the older brother of Eamon, a lad you will read about later on. Anyway, he told me I'd done well and to stick with him when we "steam the escort". And, after several attempts at this and skirmishes with the Old Bill, Plymouth's shell-shocked boys got safely to their trains and back to Devon.

Back down Smethwick High Street, as I was making my way to my bus stop, two lads that I recognised from being with us earlier, approached me and said I should turn up at New Street Station in Birmingham the next week for Nottingham. But as they walked away, one of them turned to me and said I might want to change my appearance a bit as my look attracts the Old Bill. "No offence mate!" they added. None taken, that was the skinhead days well and truly over with.

* * * * * *

Now in his 50s, Bowie has been part of scene at Albion for more than five decades and is therefore one lad many look up to. Starting in the Brummie Road End at the Hawthorns, he and his mates hooked up with lads from other areas against a backdrop of scooters, Ska and Bluebeat. He is proud of the multi-racial roots the Albion has, being mixed race and believes it's something that makes the firm stand out compared to others. Here he details how he got involved in the scene and recalls several rows in the Seventies, including battles with Forest, Leeds and Bristol City.

Bowie: I first started going in late Sixties when I lived in Newtown. Albion just appealed to me more than Villa or Blues. I liked the camaraderie and went to all the home and away games, off to Millwall, Cardiff, wherever. I think Albion have got a good crew. We're not the biggest firm but that can also be in our favour as we knew who to rely on in those days. I was aware of, and got to know, lads from Tipton, Handsworth Wood and Smethwick who were already going to matches back then. We were Brummie Road-Enders first, then we'd go to the right side of it and sing and chant "The Right Side" then when we went to the middle we'd sing "The Middle" and so on. Then, after a while, in the late Seventies or early Eighties, we decided to go in the Smethwick End and we called the Brummie Road End "The Cardboards" because you never heard anything from them during the game, like cardboard cut outs.

There was a bit of in-fighting going on as well but, generally the Brummie lads would mix with the Smethwick lads and those of us going out drinking in Birmingham were called Town Heads. We were into the Ska and Bluebeat. I was a skinhead and a suedehead and we all had scooters. I've never seen any racism down at the Albion. When

Man City were down once the National Front (NF) were dishing out their leaflets at the ground but that was a mistake, they got battered. I've never had any problems and other black lads say the same. It's always been multi-racial as far as I'm concerned. I remember one Asian lad back then, a lad called Harvey, he was a good lad. I know West Ham had Clyde Best playing for them but I think Albion were the only team who had three black players. It was unique what was happening on the pitch then. At Man United one year, I remember their fans booed every time a black player got the ball. We were friends with some Blues, who also had a mixed firm of black and white lads, and Villa lads – F.Cullen, C. Karem, Jinxy and P. Yank from the Villa's Steamers and C Crew era. My cousin is a Blues lad and we'd all knock about on our scooters and be drinking in Birmingham at the Rainbow Club on Thursday and Saturday nights - usually fighting afterwards - the Mayfair on Sundays and we were also at the Gilded Cage.

One well known Villa lad I knocked about with for a bit in the Seventies was Pete the Greek. Remember a funny story about him that he instigated about me. I was having a bath one day after playing football and was told: "Some lad wants to see you", so I went downstairs and it was Pete on his scooter. The previous day, Albion had been playing Villa and Pete and his mates were in the Brummie Road End. I warned him out when I saw him, telling him it was in his best interest to get out and he was sound with that. He said he didn't want any trouble yesterday at the game as we knew each other and fair enough what was said and that was it, he left. A few weeks later, a story started going round that he had come round and offered me out.

I happened to be in the Gilded Cage not long after with my mates when I saw him at the bar. I went up to him and asked him what was going on sort of thing. I'd heard it from different people but he kept on denying it. I thought about hitting him but didn't as it was my local and I didn't want to get banned or something as I was there all the time. I spoke to his mates too and said we'll have it then but they didn't want to know either.

We always had a good laugh wherever we went, like I said there was good camaraderie. I remember a night game at Cardiff once in the mid-Seventies. We'd gone down in cars and we met them by a bridge where it kicked off but the cops soon appeared and herded us off for the game. One lad had a false arm and the cops grabbed him by it and he said: "If you want it that bad, have it", and took it off and gave it to them.

At Arsenal on Boxing Day in 1978, about 400 of us were out. There weren't any Specials on so we went down in cars. A load of us went in the opposite end to Arsenal and were soon surrounded by them. We didn't really say anything and then some Arsenal appeared in the middle of us. My mate, Leftie, a good and game lad from Birmingham, hit one guy so, so hard and he dropped to the floor. But that was it, no one did or said anything to us after that.

At Villa one year, in fact I think it's in their book, me and Mutley and about 30 to 40 of us went in the Holte End. We were all quiet, then we started chanting and then we started getting punched all over. I had some brand new clothes on – jumper and shirt - which got ripped to shit. We got escorted round the pitch by the police to the Witton End and enjoyed the rest of the game knowing we had made a statement.

For Bristol City one Bank Holiday weekend in the late-Seventies, we went down in cars and got there early doors. I remember there were loads of Albion around. We went in a pub with Bristol in and the chanting from each firm started so it wasn't long before it went off with glasses getting chucked. It was one of their pubs and more of them appeared outside. Some of them must have thought I looked like the boxer John Conteh as they were shouting his name at me so I remembered their faces for later, especially one lad in particular wearing a cap. Anyway, we got to the ground and there was a bit of trouble during the game. Afterwards, as we drifted out we split up and went roaming around, which was what normally happened and I saw the lad in the cap with his mate. I knew as soon as he saw us he'd make a run for it so we followed him and my mate Croges walked in front of him so he couldn't escape. We were on a bridge and when Croges was in front of him we blocked him off. When he saw us he screamed. I'll always remember that, it was so funny. Croges grabbed him and I hit him a few times and threw his cap in the river below and then pretended to dangle him over the edge of the bridge. We could hear people from nearby houses shouting: "Leave him alone." We just shit him up and left him to it.

Leeds have a good firm and when we played them in the League Cup in September 1979 we got off the Special all singing and chanting and it wasn't long until they appeared. Back then I knew a couple of mates who were in the police and were out on match days on the trains and at stations. When we first got off the train, I went into a shop at the station and unbeknown to me some Leeds lads had followed me in. But the coppers I knew came in behind them and no doubt saved me from a beating. However, it was soon going off outside the station under the bridge by the main road and we heard that one Leeds lad had been run over in the trouble. We didn't know how bad or exactly where but we got a few hundred yards down the road and felt pretty cocky after the fight. We stopped off at some pubs on the way to the ground. We had a good crew out that day and had a few more skirmishes en route. I was getting pointed out in the pubs but was just saying "'Yeh, yeh?". Cocky. After the game, I was getting pointed out again and I'd spilt up from the main mob somehow and there was only a few of us together as we came out the ground. We had to run our way back to the station, it was a bloody nightmare. It felt like a personal attack on me or something. But Leeds, Man United, West Ham, Millwall were all good firms in those days.

Blackpool away in the mid-Seventies was another eventful weekend. We headed up there the day before the game for a piss up as the match was on a Bank Holiday weekend. The weather was shit and I remember we were all in a bar called Chaplins and then we headed out along the Prom. Some started diving into the sea – the tide was in – and generally messing about when we could see a crew coming towards us. They turned out to be Man United who had just come from a chippy as they were tucking in. We started nicking their chips and that started things off. We started fighting with bystanders moving out of the way and watching in horror. We were all spread out fighting and then we heard one of their lads got run over or injured by a tram. I didn't see it myself. The police appeared so me and few others left and were sat down a side street outside a B&B when the cops drove past. They got out and said they were taking us in for questioning. We got taken to a station and questioned for a couple of hours. We were taking the piss and having a laugh with them but then they kept us in. We were worried we were going to miss the match the next day but luckily they kicked us out in the morning, I remember seeing them later at the ground.

At Forest's ground back then, there was a car park joined to it, I don't know what it's like now, but people were coming off the coaches and we were all going in together. There was a good firm out. A mob of Forest came at us then but we sent them on their way. It was a good fight, quite a few casualties on the floor. Inside the ground, we were sat in one of the side stands surrounded by Forest. There was a bit of verbals going on with some of the lads we'd been fighting outside. Afterwards, me and my mates got in our cars and went for a cruise around, as was the tradition. We'd always go and have a look around. There must have been about 10 cars and vans, all full. While we were driving down this one road, we saw a bunch of Forest walking along - the ones we'd been fighting earlier. We jeered and shouted at them as we passed and they must have thought we'd gone. But further on we parked up and hid behind a building and waited to attack them. It was mayhem. I remember going after one of their lads, their main mouthpiece, up an alleyway by some houses but someone beat me to it and got to him first and went berserk. My mate got one of these washing line props and was hitting him with it in his face, a lot. He was in a bad way, it was quite full on. Everyone was quite worried after that and checking the papers and all that. But, we were back there a year later and we saw him again in the ground and he had thick lensed-glasses on this time and was pointing us out. Nothing happened on this occasion though.

Chapter Two

In The Clubhouse

*O*ne *of the founders of the Clubhouse is Snarka. As one of the authors
of this book, he is much respected and liked throughout the West Brom
firm. With a family rich in Baggies history, he was there to galvanize
the lads in the early Eighties, along with others, which led to the creation of the
first organised West Brom firm.*

Snarka: I was born in the early Sixties, the only child to good working
class parents who lived in West Brom. Dad worked in a factory as an
electrician and mom in a foundry. My family is Albion mad and we had
connections with the club through my mom's side - a great granddad
and great uncle both played for them and I still have great granddad's
England cap and Football League cap. Dad took me to my first match
when I was 14-months-old and over the next eight years or so I went
regularly with him, my nan, cousin Netty and my uncle. When I went
with my uncle, I often witnessed pitch battles as away fans tried to
take the Brummie Road End not realising that one day I would also
be invading away ends with my firm. I had a great upbringing and a
very happy childhood. Not the CV of a football hooligan to the experts.
When I started the "big school", dad allowed me to go to the games
with my mates and I went to every one with my mate Stevie Holland.
He had no interest in the violence then or now. In fact, he is a well
respected steward at the Albion and the Villa and has been for years.

We started going to all the away matches about 18 months later. My
dad would drop us off at St Francis of Assisi Church, on Friar Park in
Wednesbury, to catch the coach and would always ask the driver what

time we were due back and would then be there waiting for us when we returned. We encountered a lot of football violence then - this was the Seventies - but we never got involved, too young and frightened if truth be told. But things were about to change.

In the 1973/74 season we played Leicester City at home but Steve had the flu so couldn't go so, I went to the game on my own. While I was queuing up to pay in, I met four lads from my school. They informed me that they never paid in, just climbed over the wall at the back of the old Woodman/Rainbow stand. So, not to look like a wuss, I went with them. They dodged the police and the few stewards that were around back then and soon they were in. It took me a little longer but I finally managed it. I was buzzing all through the match expecting to be thrown out any minute. They also told me that after the match they went robbing the scarves off the away fans. When the game finished we set off back to West Bromwich but within minutes they had spotted two Leicester fans, aged about 19 or 20. "Let's get their scarves!" they said. So we began to follow them. They went down a quiet side street. They knew we were following them but they couldn't care less. We were five, 13 and 14-year-old kids. My mates made their move and surrounded them demanding their scarves. The Leicester fans laughed and told them to fuck off. A stand-off ensued, with threats being dished out on both sides. Then, for some reason that I still cannot explain today, I ran from the side and kicked the biggest one - I, along with most people then, was doing karate and had become very good. He fell to the ground. All my new mates joined in the attack and the two lads handed over their scarves to save a beating. I then cleared off expecting the police to catch me any moment.

All Saturday night and Sunday I was expecting a knock on the door but it never came. I went to school on the Monday not knowing what to expect but when I got there, I was treated like a hero by the older lads and girls. My story - probably embellished somewhat - had got round and I was even given the scarf as I had earned it. From that day I never went to another match with Steve. I started going with some of the older lads from the Yew Tree Estate in West Brom. About 20 to 30 of them would meet up with some of their brothers and older mates and called themselves the Yew Tree Vikings. They would stand in the middle of the Brummie and do battle with other factions. There was the Left Side, Right Side and Middle, a common occurrence amongst other firms around this time too. On the Right stood a mob who called themselves the Heads and they would sing stupid songs, including "One Arthur

Negus" which later became "One Cyrille Regis". On the other side would be the Tipton lot but, no one could organize them into one firm. At the away end, we had a mob called the Smethwick who would be battling with the away fans all through a match, well before segregation.

On one of my away trips, this time to Norwich, I met some lads from a rival school and we ended up sitting three to a seat as the coach was that full. They were Sutty, Wozza and Malek who, to this day, I am great friends with. They used to go in the Smethwick End and battle with the away fans. I wanted some of this so, me and a few of the lads started going in there too. The mob was led by a big bloke with a beard and he used to stand on a small fence and direct the firm. As kids we used to call him "The Beard". I found out later he was known as Budgie.

In the 1978/79 season we played Spurs who brought a huge firm. I always rated them as I used to go to Pontins as a 16-year-old with some of their young lads who were my mate's cousins. We followed their main firm down to Rolfe Street Station where Budgie led us into attack and a great battle raged. We had it toe-to-toe with them and got the upper hand. When the police came, they escorted Spurs to the station. I was with an older chap called Dixie and we were just going to jump on a bus back to West Brom when Budgie approached us and said that he'd noticed us and we'd done very well. He asked us to go for a drink with him and the rest of the main faces, including a lad called Micky Seery who later joined the ICF when he lived in London. He told all the older lads that we were game and we were welcomed into the Smethwick mob. He told us to meet him in the Blue Gates pub at the next home match. Soon, all our young lot started to meet in there and we became a sort of junior Smethwick mob.

But, this was never going to be enough so we started organizing our own coach with some daft Worcester lads – Minnie and Timmy Time Bomb (always going off). They used to pick us up at the Rotunda in Birmingham where we would often meet the Apex lads - Blues lads before the Zulus came into being. They used to give us a wide berth - we did have some right nutters. We started to go in away ends and away pubs and we soon got a reputation as Albion's number one firm. We were no better than any of the other Albion firms just more organized. Our name came when, by now, we were meeting in the Throstle Club at the back of the Rainbow Stand mainly so we could ambush away fans right outside the ground.

Some of Wolves's Subway lads were taking the piss out of us as we had not got a name - a couple of them used to come with us to some of the more tasty away games back then. But, on one occasion, Tucker, one of our main lads from Blackheath, told them "Yes we have. We're called 'The Clubhouse'", as we'd often say to each other "See ya in the Clubhouse next match." We all liked it so we agreed that's what we would be called. From then until the mid-Eighties we were a tight, organized firm of about 50 to 60 lads before our firm gave way to the Section 5 Squad. We stuck together and most if not all those friendships remain today.

There's been a lot said, mainly from Blues and Villa, about all this we were the first mixed race firm etc. Wow, what's the big deal? To put the record straight, Albion have always had black and Asian lads in the different firms, all great, solid and loyal - except for one prick who I won't bother to mention. The first main boy I ever heard of was a lad called Mutley, a black lad who's the father of young Mutley, the champion boxer. Mut' used to lead the lads, those mainly from West Brom itself and he is a really nice bloke who could have it. Then there was Bowie, a mixed race lad who would lead the Smethwick mob and has contributed to the book. He became a legend around these parts.

There are so many I could write about but most wanted to remain anonymous.

However, I do want to mention Toby and Joey Clarke who are seasoned campaigners and Asian lads like Chinda and Culla. These, along with Conner, had their Albion days cut short due to in jail terms after the Uplands battle with Villa in 2004. During the Eighties we lost a lot of black lads to the Zulus who jumped on the black-bandwagon. But, you need loyalty in this game, so fuck them. At the end of the day, if they were green, I, or anyone else wouldn't have given a toss because if you're part of the firm, be it Section 5, Clubhouse, Smethwick or whatever, it doesn't matter, you're all pissing in the same pot. So just to reiterate, we have always had black and Asian lads in our firms and always will, so what why make such a big deal about it?

* * * * * *

By the early Eighties every football club in Great Britain had a firm of like-minded individuals and at West Brom, as I've said, it was the Clubhouse. There had been gangs before - the Heads, Yew Tree

Vikings, Smethwick Mob, Tipton and the Star and Garter lot - but, the Clubhouse was Albion's first organised Casual firm. As previously mentioned, the name came about from when we used to frequent the Throstle Club behind the old Rainbow Stand (the new East Stand). We hired our own coaches with the lads from the Worcester/Droitwich and we always had the same driver, a mad Polish bloke called John and wherever we asked him to stop he obliged. The firm consisted of 50 to 60 young lads in their early 20s who went to every away match. Numbers often rose to a hundred-plus at home matches but, really only those 50-odd were really Clubhouse lads.

Two lads, John the Con and Dave the Rave, would relay information about where other firms drank or hung about - obviously way before the Internet or mobiles.

They found out by talking to workmates and pub-goers who were regulars in local firms like the Subway, Villa's Steamers/C-Crew and the Apex. They would swap information about other teams' firms and we would then plan to hit these pubs as early as possible to take them over. When home fans arrived, they would try to retake their pubs resulting in mass brawls most of the time. This was normal practice for most firms in the Eighties. We would also try to take the home fans' ends by mingling in with home supporters - you could pay at the gate then. Just before kick-off a shout of "The West Brom" would go up and a free-for-all followed rather quickly. You never stayed in there long but everyone had seen you do it. The escort round the pitch was always greeted by the away fans cheering and clapping you. We sometimes arrived by train on Friday nights or early Saturday mornings with the popular Persil cheap train ticket promotion on at the time. A couple of binmen who came with us got us the coupons off the packets.

The Clubhouse consisted of young men from West Bromwich, Wednesbury, Blackheath, Worcester, Birmingham and a couple from Leighton Buzzard. After the match we would drink in the Sandwell pub in West Bromwich which was very popular and always packed. At home games, we would meet in the Blue Gates in Smethwick where we waited for rival fans to be escorted to the ground from their trains. We would infiltrate the escort and kick it off with them. We also then went in the Throstle Club, right outside the ground to pick off the firms who evaded the police escort. The top boys were me, Tucker, Sooty, Wozza, Malak, Keil, Duzas (Twins) Big Alf the VI (Village Idiot) Twinny, Paddy, Spock, Joey and Paynne. We also had some young 16 and 17-year-olds, including Bail', Peachy, Clem, Daz and Tony Freeth who went on to form a major part of the Section 5 Squad.

The Clubhouse only lasted for four or five seasons as the Old Bill came down really heavy on us. We had banning orders and signing on at the police station on match days and constant harassment of the top boys. West Midlands Police have a terrible reputation against football firms, one which they like to live up to. An example of that is in the following story, told to me by an old Clubhouse lad, who wishes to remain anonymous. He now follows a northern club home and away, partially due to the constant harassment by West Midlands OB back in the early Eighties:

By now, the Clubhouse were sitting in the Rainbow seats. We liked to be separate from all the other firms but we also had some non-Clubhouse lads sat with us. Roughly 20 Clubhouse lads entered the ground at 2.30pm and right in front of us was about the same number of Spurs fans. Bang. We steamed straight into them for taking liberties in our seats. They scattered and took refuge on the perimeter along the pitch - no fences then. The OB soon had it all under control and as kick-off neared there were about 150 of us in the seats with Spurs along side us, separated by OB. There were also some Spurs in the top tier behind us. Fair-play, it was an impressive mob.

During the first half nothing much happened, the odd obscenity but we knew half-time would be different as the two Spurs mobs would be together. When the whistle went, we all went up the back for a beer and toilet trips and by now the Spurs mob were 300-plus and they steamed straight into us. We were really on the back foot. I saw my mate Snarka standing on his own in the middle of Spurs so I headed towards him to give him a hand, although no one touched him. Straight away our friendly West Midland OB nicked me. I eventually got a £475 fine. Remember, this was the early Eighties and you were unlucky to get £20 fine, so I was really pissed off with Spurs and wanted revenge.

I had to wait until the next season which was a night game. Again we sat in the Rainbow seats, this time about 60 of us, nearly all Clubhouse lads, and there was mob of 20 to 25 black Albion lads in the Smethwick paddock, next to the Rainbow stand.

Spurs again showed in the paddock seats but being a night game there was about 80 to 90 of them. When half-time came we all headed for the back of the stands as did the Spurs mob but, this time the OB were waiting to stop anything going off. A Spurs fan - he looked like Neville Staples from the Specials – came over and told us what was going to happen after the match. We politely told him to fuck off and carried on drinking our beer. The OB had it all sewn up as usual so nothing happened during the game and when it ended, the Clubhouse lads decided to head down Middlemore Road towards Smethwick hoping to lose the OB and catch Spurs by surprise. We were on a ramp when low and behold there was the Spurs mob, led by our dear friend Mr Staples. But, better still, not one OB was in sight.

There was no need for pleasantries as we were straight into them as were our lads who were in the Smethwick paddock who had followed them from behind. They tried to stand but to be fair they had no chance as we were all around them, hammering them from all sides. There were Spurs fans lying on the floor all over the place and I saw one Albion lad drop part of a paving slab on one Spurs fan as he was lying on the floor getting a kicking. All around me, Spurs fans were lying motionless. At least two had been slashed and Mr Staples had a bottle smashed in his face. There were plenty of casualties that day and I am sure Mr Staples and his friends remember that day fondly. Revenge is sweet.

Old Clubhouse lad

Chapter Three

Casual Antics

Snarka: From a very early age I was into my clothes and even today I still wear Prada, One True Saxon, Lacoste, Stone Island, Burberry - the latter two not so much now as every Chav in England does - Hackett, Mandarina Duck, Duck & Cover, Henri Lloyd et al. In the Sixties when I was at school, I used to follow the skinhead -suedehead fashion of the time - Ben Sherman shirts, Levi Sta-press trousers, brogues, Harrington jackets and Monkey boots - I was too small to fit into Doc Martens. Then in the early Seventies, I had platform shoes, baggy trousers and ski jumpers - not a look to be proud of. By the mid-Seventies I followed the terrace culture of Donkey Jackets and steel toe-cap boots and by the end of the decade, thanks to the Punk Rock scene, I was an avid follower of Stiff Little Fingers, Sex Pistols, Stranglers, The Clash and my all time favourite, The Jam, who wore Sixties Mod clothes which I took to. Fred Perry jumpers and sharp suits became my clothes of choice and I got into the scooter scene so, going to the match I was already dressed quite smart. I started to wear skinhead clothes like Doc Martens, braces, check shirts and flying jackets, more for practicality as riding my scooter the clothes needed to be more robust. But at the match, this look got you hassle from the OB who thought all skins/scooter boys were hooligans. As a result of this unwanted attention we saw the emergence of the Soccer Casual although we called ourselves Trendies.

We started wearing Pringle, Lyle and Scott and Cerruti 1881 jumpers, Farahs, Lacoste, Ellesse and Levi jeans, usually very light blue or bleached. The clothes and ideas came from abroad. The Scousers of Liverpool were robbing those much sought after labels as at the time they ruled the roost on the pitch in England and Europe and their scallies were soon seen around the grounds dressed in the new Casual uniform.

Our shoes were just as important as the clothes, mainly trainers with Adidas being the main brand of choice although some wore Diadora. Casual slip-on moccasins were popular for a short while but these had a habit of coming off in fights. Kagouls also became popular for a short while with the Kappa one being the sought after garment but Nike and Adidas were also popular. We started wearing golfing jackets purchased from golf clubs around Birmingham, Olton golf course being a favourite haunt of ours. As the winter set in, ski-jackets were worn more and more. I even took to wearing a Deer Stalker hat at matches - I must have looked a right prat.

Every match was a fashion parade with firms checking each other out as well as fighting each other. Looks changed from area to area with the London clubs getting the fashions before the rest of us. For a short while the OB left us alone as we didn't look like hooligans. But they soon cottoned on and now dressing in certain labels can get you hassle from OB and doormen at clubs and pubs. The culture has all but died now with everyone getting hold of these labels, mostly fake, so that some labels notably Stone Island and Burberry have been hijacked by every chav and cyber warrior wannabe which is a shame as Stone Island and Burberry have some nice clothes. Some labels are now re-emerging as older lads try to not be associated with these people with Lyle and Scott, Fila and Pringle becoming popular once more.

* * * * * * *

Albion v Wolves has always been a very special occasion for a lot of Albion fans and more so for a lot of Wolves fans. Inevitably there is more on this later in the book. However, a large number of Albion fans hate Villa more than Wolves. They're closer to us and we played them more in the Seventies due to Wolves dropping down the divisions - happy days.

In the early Eighties, we played Wolves at the Hawthorns and as usual we all met up in the Blue Gates pub in Smethwick. I would have been about 20 at the time.

We were waiting for their mob to arrive at Rolfe Street Station when they surprised us by landing at Smethwick West, the stop before, and walked the couple of miles to the Gates. They caught us completely unawares and put all the windows through at the pub. Our spotters were outside Rolfe Street waiting for them to arrive. We charged out the pub and had it toe-to-toe with them although some Albion – hanger-ons - legged it down the side of the pub. One of our main faces, Bowie, charged them on his own and was more than holding them off. In fact, they could not get anywhere near him. We backed him up as best we could as the battle raged for several minutes until the OB turned up and escorted them to the ground. After the match we all planned to get revenge and walk over Galton Bridge to confront them at Smethwick West. As we got to the bridge, we were about 60 to 80-handed and we could see Wolves waiting for us with about the same number. We charged across the bridge straight at them but straight into an ambush.

Wolves were waiting up the embankments and attacked us from all sides. There were hundreds of them. It was pitch black and raining and they threw everything at us, including a car battery. Again, Bowie stood. He was decking them left, right and centre and me and my mates - Wozza, Soot, Youngy and Malek - stood with him and his mates from Birmingham. I think they were a mixture of the Smethwick mob and the Heads from Birmingham. We backed him up as much as possible, kicking and punching everything that got in our way. We were really fighting for our lives but we stayed tight and put up a good show. It was a dangerous place to be with lads from both sides taking horrendous beatings. People were trying to get away and were slipping up the wet banks straight back into flying boots - steel toe-caps then. They were all around us. It was like Custer's Last Stand. The noise was deafening but we held our position more through instinct than anything else. Fighting to stay together and looking for friendly faces in the melee, it went on for several minutes before the OB came and scattered everyone.

Wolves claim this as one of their victories against us but, I thought we held our own against them as there were hundreds of them - Stourbridge Wolves, Subway and others. However, fair-play to them, they ambushed us good and proper. They were more organised and seemed to have a plan that they followed. To hear some Wolves talk that they smashed us all over the place, is not true. They obviously were not there. I have spoken to some old Wolves lads about that night and they said in return, fair-play to us, we stood and gave a good account of ourselves.

In the early Eighties, Albion probably had the best team we've ever had. A flamboyant Ron Atkinson was in charge of flare players like the late, great Laurie Cunningham, big Cyrille Regis, Bryan Robson, Tony "Bomber" Brown and Willie Johnstone. The football they played was a pleasure to watch. At the time, our big rivals were Aston Villa who were going for the League title. There were only a few games left when we had to play them in a night game. The stage was set for a great game of football and for weeks we had been planning to invade the Holte End, Villa's main end. I mention this game as it's in the Aston Villa book, Villains, but with a different angle on it.

As the day of the game came round, we all arranged to meet in the Temple Bar and Shakespeare in Birmingham city centre. We had a good 60 Clubhouse lads out and the plan was to walk to the ground and enter the Holte. We tried our hardest to avoid any trouble so the OB would not cotton on to our plan. On the way we saw Villa's lads, who we thought were the Steamers but they wrote in their book were probably the C-Crew. In any case, we avoided them as we wanted the bigger prize of taking the Holte. When we got to Villa Park, we'd been joined by some of the Smethwick mob which took our numbers up to between 100/150. We started to queue to get in and just as we got near the front, one of ours, Shawrie, was spotted by a Villa fan, a relative I think, who then raised the alarm. A few punches and kicks were exchanged and the OB came and rounded us all up except for eight or nine of us who managed to slip in. Once inside we were spotted straight away. We got to the top of the stairs by the toilet when Villa attacked. We had the higher ground and we managed to hold them off until the OB came to our rescue. I mention this because in their book, they fail to mention how many of us got in the ground. Yes, we never got to the terraces but we held them off for what seemed like five minutes but were probably just two or three. We were then taken out over the fence of the Holte and put in the side where all the Clubhouse lads had managed to get in. Another one of ours, Briscoe, stayed in the Holte all match and fair-play to them they left him alone.

The game itself was a tense affair but we lost to a bad back pass from Brendan Batson. After the match we all piled out and had a small row with some Villa. We all got together and decided to walk back to West Brom, about five miles, and as we got a few hundred yards up the street, we met Villa's mob. We went straight into them when all of a sudden, OB arrived on horseback clattering everyone with those long batons they had. They managed to separate the two firms and held the Villa mob against a long fence. They then let us walk past them giving them plenty of stick as really they had not troubled us at all. In their book, they say that they never rated Albion's firm. Well, how come to this day they have never showed in West Brom?

It's all about opinions but I thought we had the upper hand that day. To claim a victory against nine lads, at the most, in their main end is a bit much. Now, if we had all got in who knows..?

The last game of the 1981/2 season was at Sunderland and we all arranged to go. By now, The Clubhouse had a very tasty reputation in and around Birmingham and as usual we met outside the back of the Rotunda at about 8am. We filled up the coach with beer and spirits. Big Alf had a pack of 24, I think it was Fosters, and he began drinking them each time shouting out the number he had drunk. You must realise, Alf was only 19 or 20 at the time but as his name implies, he was a big lad.

By the time we arrived in Sunderland a few hours later he had drunk the lot. As we were travelling through the city we persuaded John, the mad Polish driver, to let us off. We all piled into the nearest boozer but were told they only served halves or wine. As we started ordering two halves at a time, Shawrie went to the toilet but two minutes later we were thrown out as he broke a mirror in there, he reckons by accident. We found another pub and had a few pints and when it was time to head to the ground, we went to the bus station to board a bus to Roker Park.

As we boarded, a big Sunderland fan asked Paddy if he could change some money for the bus. Paddy said no but he realised we were Albion fans and a few insults were exchanged before he got off. We drove to the ground and at the first stop the same Sunderland lad was there with a few of his mates. They came upstairs and sat down at the front but the big lad with them - he had a blue away top on - turned around and offered us all out. We were flabbergasted as it was just him fronting us and there were about 30 of us. A couple of lads went for him but he held them off, so everyone started trying to get to him but he was a right hard-case and was holding us off. We could only get to him one or two at a time as the bus aisle was so narrow. His mates got filled in and fled the bus but he then tried to call other Sunderland fans on the bus to get us but you could see they didn't want to know. A few tried to get up the stairs but a quick kick at the first lad's head as it popped up sent him tumbling down on to the lads trying to get up. By this time "the hardest man in the world" as we since nicknamed him, was starting to get a bit of a pummelling. So we all said to let him go and let him off the bus. He was still shouting at us but he was more upset with his mates who didn't help him. As he got off, he started to set about them and by this time the OB arrived and had a word with him and managed to calm him down. They then came upstairs and ordered us off the bus. They searched us and said they were going to escort us to Roker Park over the bridge. We expected a stroll to the ground, strutting our stuff, but we were in for a rude awakening. These OB must have been their Olympic running squad and decided to run us all to the ground with a sharp whack across the buttocks if you slowed down. They told us we were shit as they had Tottenham moving a lot quicker the week before.

When we got to the ground, they made us go in and a few of our lads - the unfit amongst us - were throwing up. When we got in, the Sunderland fans kept invading the pitch to try to get in our end. I don't think they were too happy about us going in their town. However, the match passed off without much trouble although a few of ours had run-ins with the Tipton Albion. This was common at the Albion, different firms would fight each other which, to me, stopped Albion having a real tasty firm. Tipton can get some real hard men in their ranks and at the time we had at least three if not four rival firms who just did their own thing.

On the way back to Brum, we decided to pull in at Ashby De la Zouch for a few pints and we all split up and went in different pubs. Me, Wozza, Alfie (Big Alf) and Sooty went in a pub full of Hells Angels and bikers where a pissed-up Alfie got on the table and in a mocking voice said "I bet you lot think you're hard?" Fair-play to them, they just laughed it off. After a few minutes drinking, one of ours came in the pub rounding us all up as Sam, who ran the coaches for The Clubhouse, was having some trouble with some Leicester fans. One of them had given his son, who was about 14 at the time, a dig. We all steamed over the road and about 40 Leicester fans came out the back door. There were about 15 of us as others were in the different pubs. We ran at the Leicester fans who launched a hail of glasses and bottles at us. Only Malek got hit – god knows how we avoided getting hit. We ran through a narrow archway where we clashed with them and held them off and, as more of our lads arrived, they ran back in the pub. Some of ours tried to get in the front of the pub with Big Alf putting his foot through the front window and falling over with his foot still stuck in the glass. We were trying to get him up but, as I have said he was a big lump and pissed. He kept saying "Leave me, leave me" but we managed to get him out. The Hells Angels/bikers decided to help out the Leicester fans so they attacked us as well. As we were fighting them, the Leicester fans piled out of the pub and joined in. We were up to our full contingent by then and were running them all over the place. The bikers decided to leave the Leicester fans to it and went back to their drinks. We ran the Leicester lot back in their pub and we were then told that John our driver was going so we had to get back on the coach. As we walked down the hill to the coach, the Leicester fans steamed out at us where we then ran them back into the pub. This happened two or three times with dustbins being tossed at each other.

By this time a few local plods had turned up and were trying to get us on our coach. When nearly all of us were on, the Leicester lot made one last charge at our coach. They piled into a couple of lads near the coach who pulled out their warrant cards, battered them and arrested them. They were OB on a night out. By the time more OB arrived, the ones who were just having a drink put all the blame on the Leicester fans. Although they did nick Big Alf for criminal damage. We tried to change clothes with him when they came to identify him but nothing would fit him so he was taken away protesting his innocence. We were given a police escort out of the town and told never to come back.

In 1982 Swansea City were in the top flight of English football – the old Division One – when we were due to play them. The Clubhouse hired a coach as usual with our normal driver, Polish John - an unsung Clubhouse legend. We set off to Wales and stopped off for a drink in Newport, I think. We were drinking with loads of rugby supporters and had a great time with not a hint of trouble before we all got back on the coach and headed to Swansea. As we neared the ground, we passed a pub full of Jacks who came flying out hurling glasses and abusing our coach. This prompted us to shout to John the driver to let us off the coach. We all piled off and charged them back into the pub and they tried to lock the doors but we just charged right in. They carried on running straight out the back doors and away.

We were buzzing and decided to walk to the ground, the old Vetch, sampling the beers on the way in a few of the local pubs and gaining a few Albion lads at each one. We arrived at the ground at about 2.45pm about with about 100-plus. The Swansea lads in their end were inviting us in as we passed and it seemed rude not to take them up on their offer so we started to pay in. A lot of the non-Clubhouse Albion decided to just carry on to the away end so roughly 40 of us went in. We gathered

on the lower level as the Swansea lads ran to the terracing, no doubt
to inform their boys we were in. Soot' asked me where we were going
to stand as we entered the terracing and I could see their boys right in
the middle of the stand so like a idiot I pointed to them and said there.
We went right to the back of them and stood behind them. As this was
going on their attention was taken up with the legendry Welsh boxer,
Roy Jones, who was being introduced to the crowds. He'd just fought
Tommy "The Hitman" Hearns in what was described at the time as the
fight of the century. A shout of "The West Brom" went up and every
one of them scattered leaving just the 40 of us in their end, right in the
middle of the stand. Not a good place to be for what happened next.

We were giving it large, shouting "Come on you Welsh Bastards"
when out of nowhere, massive men in their 30s and 40s appeared from
out of the crowd. They were baying for blood and us Englishmen
who had dared to come in their end and steamed into us. We
were youngsters, teenagers and lads in our 20s and we were now
surrounded. We fought our way to the front to get out whilst trying to
stay together to look after ourselves. Bernie, a black lad who was with
us, was a particular target not because he is black but because he had
his England top on. All around Clubhouse lads were getting a right
battering as were a few Welsh who mixed with the tastier scrappers.
We all managed to get to the front with not too many injures and piled
onto the pitch where the OB rounded us all up and escorted us round
to where the Albion fans were. We were treated like conquering heroes
and cheered all round the pitch and patted on the back as we were put
in amongst them.

On the downside, seven Clubhouse lads including, Soot, Tucker
and Big Alfie were nicked along with a couple of Swansea lads, who
informed our lot that not even Cardiff were daft enough to come in
their end. That summed up the Clubhouse in my opinion. Not the
hardest or biggest firm but definitely one of the gamest and, still to
this day, when you meet other old Clubhouse lads that's the first story
they talk about.

PART TWO

Chapter Four

Next Generation – The Section 5 Squad

B *y the early-to-mid-Eighties, football hooliganism was huge, with episodes of violence across the country hitting the headlines every week. This prompted some lads to drop out or settle down or just take more of a back seat inevitably leading to a new generation coming through and making their mark.*

This was also true of West Brom. With the Clubhouse beginning to fade Tony Freeth, slightly younger than the lads from that era, became jointly responsible for creating and organising the latest firm to hit the Hawthorns terraces: The Section 5 Squad. The title was taken from the charge many lads found themselves landed with after being arrested for trouble at matches.

As one of the authors of this book, Tony writes about a trip to Rotherham, one of his first with the Clubhouse, an almighty battle with Man United in the Blue Gates, involving young and old and, how a visit to Leicester saw him impress which eventually led to him being one of several to front the next wave of lads.

Tony: By now I was hooked on football and what it entailed. All I could think about and talk about was football violence. I wanted to learn from anybody who was something up the football - firms, clothes, everything to do with it. I really did become infatuated with it all. One of my first trips with the Clubhouse, although it was coming to a close, was to Rotherham for an FA Cup game in January 1984.

About 60 to 70 of us met up at New Street Station and caught the 9.30am to Sheffield. When we arrived, we were met by the Old Bill who quickly rounded us up and gave us an escort. They were very kind in taking us to a pub right opposite the home end, where we spent the next couple of hours. Can you believe that? Well, after a few sherbets the pull of the home end was too much for us and about 40 of us, in two and threes, paid in the Rotherham end. Once in, we all had the same idea and made our way to the end where we'd been told their boys stood. When we were all together a huge cry of "The West Brom" went up and running battles started. In truth it wasn't much of a battle. No sooner had we started punching the Yorkshire lads, they ran in all directions. It was mayhem as they ran all over each other to get away. They tried to make a little show once the Old Bill started to lead us around the pitch and back to the thousands of Albion behind the goal, and a heroes welcome. I can still vividly remember a certain Albion defender, who shall remain nameless, who was about to take a throw-in as we walked past. He just looked at us, before saying with a broad grin "Go on lads!" Nothing happened afterwards, they were no where to be seen. I think they knew they'd bitten off more than they could chew - there were even more of us together after the game - and they never came near us.

A few months later, we were playing Man United and I caught the early morning train from Old Hill, where I was living at the time, to Smethwick Rolfe Street. I had arranged to meet one of the older Clubhouse lads, Carlow, in our main pub which at the time was the Blue Gates on Smethwick High Street. I arrived very early, about 10am and found the large pub almost empty. I looked around and couldn't see Carlow so I stood at the bar and ordered myself a lager. I took my change and scanned towards the main double doors of the pub where to my surprise a hefty body of lads were coming through the door. They seemed to fill the entrance up very quickly and then moved to the bar. The worrying thing was that there was not one face amongst them that I recognised. I stood frozen to the spot. A lad next to me, with a sizeable scar from cheek to earlobe, asked me in a southern accent "Is this West Brom's pub?" I just nodded and he didn't say a lot more as the group carried on ordering their drinks. One bloke in particular caught my eye, a strapping lad, around 6ft 2 and probably around 15 or 16 stone with thinning hair on top. He looked a tough-nut for sure and I nicknamed him "Tank". It was obvious this group, numbering about 40, were Man United but they had just made a very big mistake. Not only was this our main pub but, of all the places to sit. They were in an area that is a dog-leg if you like, off the main room of the pub. It had one entrance/exit and once they were sat in there, they had only one means of escape which was back into the main part of the pub. I thought, if they stay they're trapped.

As time passed, more and more Albion lads, young and old, both Casuals and normal fans came into the pub. Some of the first of our lot to arrive were not aware of the Man United presence. The Gates is a massive pub and the group couldn't be seen unless you were on that side of the pub. Over the next couple of hours the beer flowed, on both sides, with some mingling and chatting to one another. Some however, were plotting things of the nasty kind. I was aware that "Tank" kept muttering things to his associates while continually glancing in my direction. I was doing a similar thing but a bit more subtle. This was a very strange situation as everyone on both sides knew what was going to happen it was just a case of when.

Neither side seemed in a hurry but as time crept by something had to give. The pool tables in the pub were emptied of the balls and the cues seemed to be missing, strangely enough. The bar staff were very supportive of the local lads and started handing out darts. Everyone seemed to be arming themselves, some even with hockey sticks and all of the pub's glasses, bottles, ashtrays, chairs and tables. Anything lads could get their hands on.

The time bomb continued to tick. I glanced over at the once chirpy Southerners and it seemed their mood had changed. They were now, it seemed, very tense indeed and quiet. More and more Albion lads started to stand by the exits and toilets. Man United now had no escape. At about 2pm it was time for the talking to stop. Surprisingly enough, they initiated what was to come by chanting "Fuck off West Brom". My God, I have never before or since witnessed in a pub what happened next. In the film Gladiator, the phrase "Unleash hell" is said in first few scenes in the forest and this was us unleashing our hell. Glasses, bottles, ashtrays, coins and bits of wood filled the air and seemed to find every target they were aimed at. For a good 20 to 30 seconds they could not return fire due to the sheer volume of missiles flying at them. Then, the already bloodied Man United received severe punishment up close and personal from lads wielding hockey sticks, more glasses, pool balls, darts, fists and boots. It was relentless and the noise was deafening.

They tried to escape but failed. They just could not manage to get out of the area they had foolishly sat in. At least six of them were glassed in and around the face and screams filled the air and blood was everywhere. Albion showed no mercy. The cheeky bastards had come into our pub without an invite and they were now paying a heavy price for it. It's a real struggle to accurately describe the carnage. It was brutal.

The whole affair lasted approximately five to 10 minutes and believe me, these Man United lads were severely written off. There was so much blood and that part of the pub was wrecked. Their cries for mercy fell on deaf ears and they were attacked over and over again. Bodies were strewn all over the place. The police stormed into the pub eventually and closed it down. The damage was done. Three ambulances were used to ferry the half-dead United lads to hospital.

The events of this day started a rivalry between us and them. The following season, leading up to a summer home game with them we had a good idea Man United would try the early-bird tactic again. Sure enough, at about 11am they turned up at Smethwick Rolfe Street Station, around 60-handed. Tweed jackets and flared jeans were in evidence. But the difference this time was that we were prepared. We had over a 150 lads waiting for them in and around the Blue Gates. The moment we caught sight of them we sprinted en masse towards them - Mancs, Brummies, Cockneys - whoever they were they did not even attempt to front us. They turned and ran and we didn't get anywhere near them.

A third incident with them at ours came about from a firm of Man United coming from the area of the Talbot Inn pub further up the High Street. Both firms headed into each other and to be fair we outnumbered Man United two-to-one. The numbers difference soon showed and then the police came in between us to stop the fighting. The retreating Man United firm was glad of the police presence. I am not saying these Man United firms were their actual firm of the time in fact, I am pretty sure they were not however, they were lads/Casuals on our manor and they were up for it so in our defence, you can only do what is in front of you. That's exactly what we did on all three occasions I have mentioned. Without doubt, the Blue Gates incident is one of, if not the, bloodiest fight I have witnessed in the confines of a pub.

Message to "Tank", if you are reading this I was the lad in the BJ Fila top. You said you were going to do me, you did not. In fact you never got near.

* * * * * * *

Snarka: Before a game at Leicester in 1984, we'd heard Wolves had come unstuck there as their Baby Squad were building quite a reputation in the Midlands by the mid-Eighties. One of ours, John the Con, had been talking to some Wolves Subway lads about how they were lured down a side street and ambushed by the locals, their favourite trick apparently. So when we played them, we arranged to meet at 9.30am at New Street Station in Birmingham where we boarded the train to Leicester, 60-handed.

As I've said, the Clubhouse was a multi-racial firm with black, Asian and white lads all included. Other firms claim they were also multi-racial but I don't remember it that way as most firms were quite right wing at this time. The Asian and black lads knew a little boozer in some right dodgy area of Leicester so we all piled in there whilst some of the young lads went on the rob around the local shops. We were getting visits from the local gangsters who couldn't believe that there were white lads in this area with black and Asian mates. But to be fair, they spoke to some of ours and just left us alone. The year before though, some of our black lads had suffered a torrid time here.

As kick-off approached, we decided to head to the ground. There were maybe 80 to 100 of us by then. We met some young Leicester lads who tried to get us to go down a side street to a pub where they said the Baby Squad would be but we knew their trick. So we stayed at the top of the road and beckoned the few Leicester lads on show to come to us. As they could see we weren't going to fall for their plan, they started to appear out of their hiding places, two side streets just before the pub. As we neared Filbert Street, the old home of Leicester, the OB were on to us like a shot trying to hold us until they could escort us into the away end. Me and Tucker and a few of our main lads managed to evade them but we were down to about 30 odd by now. As we got outside one of the main stands, trying to look inconspicuous, we intended to go in their end but we got spotted by some Baby Squad following us. They steamed across at us. Well, with the stand right behind us we had no choice but to stand our ground - not that it ever entered my head to get on my toes. I was never the hardest man but something inside me just could never see any danger, something I have lived to regret over the years. A stand-off ensued with insults being exchanged. Tucker looked at me and smiled and I knew then we were charging. A shout of "Clubhouse!" went up and we just steamed in catching them totally unawares. They turned and ran while a few of their gamer lads stood and took the beating. The OB were onto us straight away. In those days they would give you a smack in the mouth and told to behave. They rounded us all up and took us into the away end. We had a good battle but were disappointed as we were trying to get in their main end.

In the ground we met up with the rest of the Clubhouse and Albion lads and were buzzing about what had gone on. The rest of the lads who were not involved wanted some of this so couldn't wait for the match to end. Some of the younger lads in particular had done themselves proud and now formed a formidable part of the Clubhouse. When the game ended, we were first out to do battle with the Baby Squad but the OB were having none of it. They laid on a sizeable escort back to the station. As we reached a junction, the Baby Squad made their move and came charging around the corner at us. We stood expecting maybe 90 to 100. We clashed with them but they just kept coming, there were hundreds of them. It was like a Wild West brawl with everyone fighting toe-to-toe with the OB trying to regain order with dogs and horses.

In amongst the fighting one of my mates Sago, he wasn't a Clubhouse lad he just liked to have a fight and a good time, had his tooth knocked clean out. You could hear him shouting "Stop, stop!" which unbelievably everyone round him did and he found his tooth. He then ran to a corner shop for some glue and stuck it back in, much to everyone's amusement. The OB managed to regain control and charged the Baby Squad back down the street. Their firm that day after the match was one of the biggest and gamest I have ever seen. I was glad the OB chased them off as they just kept coming and coming, there must have been 500 to 600 of them. I think they were mad as we hadn't fallen into their trap but, I think we held our own. We were buzzing all the way home to West Brom but, more importantly some of our younger faces had come of age.

Tony: As Snarka has said, this day was one where he and others noticed that the younger lads, including me, were starting to come through. I remember as we approached the ground, the police clocked us and started the usual stop and search tactic and before you know it, you're split up in different directions. I kept a watchful eye on the main faces and tagged along with the main firm of the time, Snarka, Tucker and the Shaw brothers. I must admit to feeling quite nervous as we turned the corner with a crew no bigger than 40. We walked past one of the home ends on the side and before you could bat an eyelid, lads just seemed to come from every direction and had us backed up against the wall of the ground. This was their boys, the Baby Squad, and by the look on their faces they weren't going to let us off the hook. The usual stand-off took place, with screams of "Come on then!" A tall, skinny black lad came out a bit further than the rest and as everyone surged forward something just clicked in me and I cracked him right in the mouth. He went down under a hail of kicks as Albion steamed in and had the East Midlanders on their toes. The fact we attacked with such ferocity left them totally shell-shocked. We chased them down catching a few of the braver ones and battering them. As you could imagine, the arriving police were in no mood to fuck about and quickly rounded us up and led us to the away end.

We were well pumped up and buoyant as we met up with the rest of our firm inside the ground. It was at this stage I noticed some of the older lads who usually didn't really acknowledge me, start to do so. A few asked me my name and I even heard one of them tell another how I did that Leicester lad. I felt full of adrenalin and confidence, as we started to watch the game. After the game, if we thought that was it for the day we were to very much mistaken. As we made our way to the station under a fairly heavy police escort, one of the biggest mobs of lads I'd seen at the time came running full pelt towards us from one side of a crossroads. Everyone clashed at the same time, us, the police and Leicester. There were fists, boots and truncheons flying all around, people running all ways, screaming, shouting, the noise was deafening. Police dogs and coppers on horseback tried to regain control and eventually did with the Baby Squad backing away.

We got back to the station on a high. Twice that day we'd been heavily outnumbered and twice we'd come out on top. Everyone was buzzing on the journey back home, more importantly for me a lot of the main faces had seemed to have taken to me.

Chapter Five

Central News

Tony: By 1985, we'd built up a relatively good but, mainly young firm. A lot of the old Clubhouse lads had faded away, and it was also the time of the ICF documentary "Hooligan". For weeks we'd been trying to think of a name for our boys as every other firm seemed to have one when one of my good friends, a game lad called Joey Clarke, came up with "Section 5 Squad". He took it from the charge relating to football disorder at the time. We loved it and that was that. Calling cards and the like were made and it soon stuck.

Soon after that, in November 1985, we drew Villa in the League Cup. A good firm of around 150 had actually met up in a pub in Aston called the Albion, which is less than half-a-mile from their main pub at the time, the Manor Tavern. Strangely enough, we were unaware of this anyhow, nothing happened at the game but after a 2-2 draw we came out firmed-up to be met by one of their top boys, Gary Little. He was to later become a friend of mine before he was tragically killed in a building site accident. He led us back towards Aston and fair-play, not one of our lads said anything to him. When we got by the Manor Tavern, which lay at the bottom of a slight incline, he asked us to wait at the top of the road and he trotted back to the pub. When Villa came out, we steamed down towards them. Punches and kicks were exchanged and Villa backed off towards the pub. When Little came swinging a piece of wood about, shouting for Villa to stand, that changed everything that night. Villa came charging back. There seemed to be more of them now, two marine flares were shot straight at us at head-height and to be fair, they just kept on coming. Although a few of us tried to stand, panic had set in and they had us on our toes. Within seconds, mounted police and vans galore charged between us and marched us back into the city centre. We were gutted. People were arguing and blaming each other but we had the replay a few weeks later to make amends.

In the week leading up to it, it was decided it would be a good idea to meet in the New Inns pub on the Soho Road in Handsworth as Villa always came that way - even now to this very day they've never come into West Brom or any of our pubs. A few lads got together the night before and made about a dozen petrol bombs and hid them in the bushes on Island Road, the road to our ground, which Villa had always taken when playing us. Nothing happened before the game, but we weren't that concerned as we knew they'd definitely be walking right past the bombs after the game. About 10 minutes before full-time, several of us made our way to Island Road and waited. We were high on adrenalin and we'd told plenty of our firm just to get to this road and ignore Villa until then. It was payback time but, as both sets of fans left the Hawthorns, our pleas had fallen on deaf ears as a few scuffles took place right in front of the Old Bill who quickly rounded up the Villa. And, for the first time ever took them past Island Road and straight down the Soho Road. We were distraught. All the plans had gone pear-shaped. In desperation, loads of us got on a number 74 bus and past the Villa firm and hid down a canal embankment, just past the Hockley flyover. As they got near enough, we came running out and straight at them. Villa ran everywhere before the police fucked us off, but they never knew till now just how lightly they got off.

A few months later, in February 1986, our newly-formed firm was to face Blues but, in fact we got absolutely hammered - literally - by Zulus brandishing hammers. A very small but game firm of around 30 took on the Blues firm in their own backyard, outside the Crown pub in John Bright Street in Birmingham city centre, as confirmed by Walton in the Zulu book. He gave a very honest account of what went on in our revenge attack the next time we'd played each other. Although, I did think Cola, one of our lads, was more accurate about the number of Blues than Walton was. Still, it's a crackin' book, but overall, I did think we would have got more of a mention than we actually got.

On the morning of playing Blues at theirs it was freezing in fact, the game was rumoured to have been called off so at first our crew only numbered about 20. We got on the bus to Birmingham city centre and made our way to the normal watering holes Albion frequented when in town – the Shakespeare, Temple Bar and the Iron Horse, where we met a few more of our lads having a drink. I remember thinking as we passed around our new Section 5 calling cards, that with so few out it would probably be best if the game was called off. After an hour or so, JL, Franklyn and Gav P, decided they were going for a quick drink elsewhere but said they'd be back shortly.

I had a quick count of heads and we totalled 29 - 32 including the trio who had just departed. The mood was, let's not go out of our way for it today as they are bound to come across us instead. We just didn't have the numbers. Meanwhile, the three lads had gone into Kaleidoscope, which, for those of you not familiar with Blues, was a Zulus stronghold. Apparently they had a drink or two before someone asked them who they were. As bold as brass they said "West Brom" and then both sides flew into one another. The three of them battled like good 'uns, giving as good as they got before throwing fire extinguishers to make a final charge to get out from where they were trapped and back to us. Mad, brave, crazy, take your pick but there wouldn't be many lads that would have done what they did. Quality, I'm sure you'd agree.

Buoyed by our returning heroes, we decided to make a move and went up to a couple of more pubs then beer and adrenalin took over as we started out for the Zulu quarters. Can't remember who thought of this though, maybe JL or Franklyn fancying round two? The first pub we came to was the Crown. We ran into a few stragglers and ran them back into the pub and smashed a few of the windows in. We then turned and bounced up the road towards Kaleidoscope and fuck me, they came steaming out of there full-pelt down the road towards us - what seemed likes hundreds of them shouting their famous Zulu chant. It wasn't an ideal situation to be in but we stood firm. JL shouted "Stand! Stand!" They seemed to come over the top of us, to the side of us and right through us. We held out as best we could but a couple of their lot were tooled up, one catching JL across the head with a claw hammer. We were getting hammered, literally, and we ran for it in all directions. They ran us through the markets all the way to Digbeth where the Old Bill stopped us. I've never been so happy to see the police in all my life - that was until one of them nicked me. Anyway, Albion got an escort to the ground and that was the end of the suicide mission for the day.

With regard to the Apex-Zulu book by David George, he says they saw about 70 of us come bouncing up the road to them. In his defence, there were a load of shoppers about but 70? I wish it had of been because I don't think we'd have budged had that been the case. I've always thought of us as a bit of a thorn for Blues as we have taken a few liberties but, so have they. All in all, a lot of Blues and Albion lads get on. One of my best mates, Malcolm Melvin used to run with the Zulus. When Blues have played Albion, something has usually occurred but when we used to be on New Street going away nine times out of ten so were they but nothing untoward was ever said. On the whole the Zulus were "the firm" in the Midlands but, I would say they have a healthy respect for us.

* * * * * * *

The two firms met again a few months later. The Zulus had had a big success at Pompey prior to them playing at the Hawthorns and a feeling of invincibility existed within the firm as so few had taken on so many down there. They assumed a similar outcome was likely at West Brom but, the lads wanted revenge after their previous meeting in Birmingham city centre. A few Zulus went on ahead of the majority of their firm and settled in the Lewisham pub before a mighty battle took place in the town centre resulting in a Blues lad being stabbed. Walton admits "they spanked us silly" and underestimated them and, although it went off again after the match, he feels to Blues' advantage, the damage had been done.

Joey, one of the later Clubhouse and early Section 5 lads, was fingered as the guy responsible for the stabbing. It's an accusation he refutes and he wanted to tell his version of events.

Joey: Blues were doing well and had a good reputation by the time we were due to play them in November 1986. There were about 200 of us out by 10am, Section 5 and Clubhouse lads. Two of my mates, Leroy and Stuart, who are Blues, came down to have a look and they got wasted in the pub. A bit later Blues settled in the Lewisham and we started walking to the ground. They came out of the pub and then started chucking tomatoes, leeks and cabbages whatever from a fruit and veg' store next to the pub but we soon clashed in the road. They said in their book, there were about 30 of them but it was more like 60. There was only one copper on a bike nearby with about 300 or more lads fighting in the road. He soon got knocked off. A flare was let off by us lot and there were bodies of Blues lads on the floor.

I don't know who got stabbed but it wasn't by me but I got the blame. I think other lads know who did it. I didn't even see it happen I just heard about it later. My mate was the one who took him to hospital. There was no way it was intentional that you go to stab another black guy, usually you're getting targeted. After the fight we went up to the ground. There was trouble in the town centre after, a stand-off by Apollo 2000 in a side road. We pushed them back, they pushed us back but the police appeared and intervened and stopped it. Blues came back up later on but we had dispersed by then.

On the Monday I went to court to see my mates who had been arrested for the trouble. I was walking into town afterwards and saw some lads around and then saw Wally (Walton) behind me, I must have been followed. I didn't see him by a phone box as he says but he grabbed me and put a knife to my throat. If he had the bottle he would have done me but he didn't. If one of their lads got cut maybe he should? But, I pushed him off and ran off.

Overall, some of our lads went with Blues, the Handsworth Albion lot, but we were all friends. Blues were more active and doing more earners. I think they are Albion at heart but they never came back. I wasn't tempted, I am always West Brom.

I dropped out for a few years after getting blamed for the stabbing. It upset me and about three weeks afterwards I heard that guys were coming to West Brom looking for me, ready to kidnap me and take me away. It put me off hearing that I was going to be put in a body bag and all that. I just wanted to leave it. Maybe I got blamed because I was a bit of a face and well known to some? I came back out again in the Nineties because I was missing it and went back on the coaches. I'd still see people but never go to matches.

One other thing I'd like to say is about Villa and respect to Garry Little, (RIP). Three of us took a hammering at Villa in the Nineties and he stepped in to save us. It was a night game and some Albion left and it was just us three fighting about 20 Villa. Garry saw me, picked me up off the floor and said "Come with me" so I just wanted to say big respect to him for that.

* * * * * * *

Tony: Coventry at theirs in April 1985 is a day that many of us won't forget in a hurry. Home or away, it's fixture that always went off so plans were made to meet at New Street to get over there nice and early. All went according to plan as dozens of lads settled in the Three Tons pub in the city centre. Although our numbers weren't as great as expected due to a few dozen of our lot going to Wembley with Halesowen for the FA Vase Final it was still a good crew, full of experience. As the time ticked by, people knew it wouldn't be long before Coventry would find us and sure enough it wasn't. The familiar sound of "They're here!" went up and the two firms clashed outside the boozer. Albion charged into the paved area outside and Coventry then ran off, simple result? Unfortunately not for one of our lot.

You see, one of our lads, who I will call Pat, carried on chasing them. Pat being big, strong and very brave obviously had tunnel vision and hadn't noticed the fact that the rest of us had given up the chase as the police had also arrived. The brave Cov lads, seeing their fearless and unsuspecting victim alone and stranded, turned and basically kicked and punched him but even worse, slashed him to pieces with craft knives. One cut started just above his temple right the way down to his jaw line, with further slash wounds across various parts of his anatomy including his back, hips and legs. It was a truly horrific and cowardly attack. To Pat's credit, he bravely fought on and eventually the heroic acts of the Cov lads ended and they dispersed.

By now, everyone was aware of what had gone on and the Old Bill to their credit got him sorted and off to hospital pretty quickly. He survived but still shows the scars today. Very fucking brave – Cov run off from a firm but one man on his own, no problem for Cov, none at all. Obviously there was no way were we going to let that go. It was proper horrible to see and it stays with you. Next time we played them away, about 80 of us met up very early to get the train from New Street, only this time about half of us carried blades. We were well pumped-up and revenge for Pat was definitely talked about. We holed up in a pub on the Ringway and started having a few drinks. Many of us younger lads drank outside as it was a red-hot day. I think it was about 1.30pm when they showed up, only about a dozen of them. To the young lads outside, this was our chance. As they bounced around showing their blades and beckoning for us outside to come and have it, the cry went up of "We've got them this time". Almost spontaneously, everyone outside pulled out their blades and ran full pelt into them. As you can imagine they ran for their lives. We chased them for quite a way but the Old Bill got to us first and that was that, for now.

The police got us all out the pub and marched us towards the ground and we then went to another pub. We were in there no longer than 15 minutes when the windows got smashed. We again ran out to find Coventry on their toes and finally the police made us go to the ground. Inside, we sat next to some of their "boys" separated only by a fence. Insults were regularly traded and several times references were made to the attack on Pat, which only served to make the atmosphere more and more ugly. As full-time approached we told them in no uncertain terms that we were up for it and then we left but when we got outside, nothing. The general mood was that Coventry didn't want to play. We kept walking towards the city centre and after a while we came to pub called the Vauxhall with lads hanging around. We vastly outnumbered them so it wasn't any surprise to discover they didn't want to know. But, after a minute all hell broke loose as their numbers were swelled by lads returning from the game. They quickly got their act together and now we were outnumbered as they charged us. After brief exchange of, funnily enough, only fists, we had it on our toes as they overpowered us but cue the maniac that is Mickey Rodgers. As we were backing away, Mick charged through us and fists on overdrive he ran straight into the oncoming onslaught. I remember he got caught up in amongst them as they ran and had Cov lads hanging off him. We just couldn't believe what was happening. It certainly slowed us all down. He was punching, kicking and snarling…that was Mick. They couldn't get him down. In fact, they seemed to be hitting themselves more than him.

As we made efforts to get our brave warrior back, the Old Bill came steaming in through in all directions and it was over as quickly as that. All-in-all, the day wasn't a success but none-the-less eventful. But as for Mick, what can you say? Over the next few years, we had minor clashes with Cov' but to be honest they kept turning up at the Blue Gates pub in Smethwick, only to turn and run like fuck to get away from us. I just hope the lads that done Pat have had a torrid time in life ever since.

Did we ever get revenge for him? Of course we did but that has to stay a secret I'm afraid.

* * * * * * *

To be honest, I couldn't think of anything in recent times to write about Forest and then Big Jon informed me that they had done a book and claimed we never turned up against them. I wasn't surprised, another firm embarrassed by us and not wanting to admit it – "Who? West Brom? Nah, Wankers". So after a few hours of thinking about them, I've remembered some little offs and one particular piss-take by us.

In March 1984, we travelled to Beeston and had a few jars close to the bus stations. Some more of our lads, mainly black lads, were due in on the next train so we piled on to the bus to the city centre, just about all fitting on board. Unfortunately the Old Bill clocked us and were keeping tabs on the bus. Somehow we managed to give them the slip and started to pile in a pub fairly close to the train station. It was then a firm of about 60 lads came steaming down towards us. They thought we were Forest and we thought likewise about them but they were our lads who had come on the later train. Now we did have a proper, good firm to take on the mighty Forest.

We'd all been in the pub about 10 minutes when the local police came in demanding that everyone from Wolverhampton had to leave. Can you imagine the reply?! Anyway, they got us onto the pavement outside which made the mob look massive. Some lads managed to slip the escort and went on the rob and got some really smart trackie tops which were the biz' at the time. We didn't see anything of Forest on the way to the ground so we all paid into the seats in their new stand, at the time, on the side where we knew their lads would be. Obviously the police were aware of the potential situation and made sure we were all in the section next to the away support. By now we'd picked up other lads en route to the ground and our numbers swelled to close on 200 - bit hard not to spot Mr Forest author. Anyway, they came into the seats next to us and they too had a great crew. The game ended which we lost and you could see their firm making their way out. As the Old Bill kept us in, we thought that was that but as we came out, for some reason that I'm still scratching my head at, the police let us walk down towards the Trent end, left alongside the river and back towards the bridge right where the Forest mob were stood. As a walk turned into a canter, we approached the foot of the bridge, heart racing and stomach churning. I just couldn't see how this was going to happen. It didn't look like the police were going to bother stopping us. As the two firms met in the middle of the road on the bridge the usual screams went up, sirens blurred and horses' hooves clattered on the tarmac. Guess what? Forest did one. Simple as that.

Our gob-smacked crew chased on but the scattering Forest firm were replaced with dozens of not very happy looking plod. We were absolutely buzzing and taking the piss big time out of any Forest lads hanging about and there were a few. I don't know, perhaps they thought we were West Ham, not West Brom? Could be an excuse used I suppose. Anyway, Mr Forest author, those 200 lads on the bridge were West Brom. Over the next few times we met them, there was the occasional 10 second skirmish but that was about it, nothing fantastic.

What they wrote about us in their book was the time when a couple dozen of them went in the Brummie Road. If you are not familiar with the layout of our ground, none of our boys occupy that particular part of the ground. On this and most days we were housed in the bottom seats in the Rainbow stand. If you're sat in the Brummie Road, it's the stand to your left. When Forest went one up, they celebrated and got taken along the side of the pitch past where we're all sitting with loads of stewards and Old Bill blocking our route to get to them. The game was held up as we tried frantically to get to them and they kept drifting further and further on to the pitch and away from us. They didn't look they wanted to know. After the game, hundreds of Albion hung around for them but they wouldn't come near. So, Mr Shippy (aka Boatsy) what have you exactly done against us? I'll tell you, apart from playing up in the shirters-end, fuck all.

Chapter Six

London Firms

Tony: To be honest, with the exception of Millwall, no real major battles have happened between us and firms from the capital but, that's mainly down to West Midlands Police swamping everywhere when West Ham, Spurs, Arsenal or Chelsea came to the Hawthorns. There have been some episodes of trouble though, the most memorable with Millwall.

We drew them in the League Cup in the 1984/85 season and all our coaches were smashed up and the police wouldn't let us out of the Den till after 10pm. We had a torrid time so when the second leg came around us youngsters – those who went on to form the Section 5 Squad - decided we had to be prepared for them. This was still in the Clubhouse days with us younger ones towing the line behind them. Millwall caused a shock beating us 3-0 in the first match as they were in Division Three and we were in the First. We all used to sit in the bottom tier of the old Rainbow stand and they brought thousands although we never saw anything of them before the game. There was a firm of them next to us but it was a surprise when we heard "Millwall, Millwall" and that Viking chant they used at that time from the top tier behind us. We had a good sized mob out and along side us was an equally good sized mob of Millwall. They came at us and we drove them back and then we steamed into them and were getting the upper hand. It spilled out onto the perimeter of the pitch which, for us was the worst thing that could have happened as the Millwall firm in the upper tier could now see what was going on below and they came flooding out over the top of the executive boxes. They dropped down like solider ants, dozens and dozens of them. With their firm considerably increased, we just couldn't cope and we ran across the pitch. The Old Bill were all over them by now and they herded us into the Woodman corner on the side of the Brummie Road and Rainbow paddock.

I thought we had done really well until we were overwhelmed and at that time, they were probably the top firm in the country. The police also had a torrid time after the match especially as we won 5-1. Millwall just ran amok in the streets adjacent to the Hawthorns, smashing everything in sight. The incident was well documented in the press at the time but was overshadowed by the riot at the Luton and Millwall game otherwise I think it would have made national headlines.

Arsenal

Arsenal always brought huge firms to the Albion but the police always seemed to keep us apart. One year however, about 1985 I think, we were milling around our main pub, the Blue Gates in Smethwick - remember the metal pedestrian bridge?

Nearly an hour after the match there were about 40 of us tops, in little groups scattered about when someone shouted "Fucking hell. Look!" There must have been about 200 Gooners walking, very casually, over the bridge towards us. The bridge is less than 100 yards from the pub and everyone went into a bit of a flap as they picked up their pace down the stairs and onto the pavement. To be fair, some of us stood but most had gone. Just as we were about to clash, the police turned up in a van and somewhat half-heartedly drove into them. The Old Bill seemed to appear from many streets adjacent to where we were and rounded them up and I must admit, I thought we were fucking lucky.

I'm quite familiar with Gooners as we had a black lad who got in with their main lads. He was one of my best pals at the time but he doesn't want me to mention his name, I'll call him Rob. I occasionally went with him to watch Arsenal and one of their top boys, a black guy called Spencer Richards from Cricklewood who became a good pal of mine. Spencer used to stop at Rob's in West Bromwich every other week and we sort of adopted him and he'd come with us to a few games. He said he was surprised how many good lads Albion had. In fact, it was Albion who took Arsenal to the Manor Tavern when they played Villa one year and the Gooners totalled it. To this day, I see Arsenal as my second team, if there is such a thing.

Chelsea

I only caught sight of their firm once at the Albion and fuck me, it was impressive but the police were all over them and when they came to town nothing much happened. Although I was banned, I know we took a firm of about 30 on the train to theirs for a Cup game in the mid-Nineties but again, nothing happened. I think we got lost in the crowds.

West Ham

I remember we played West Ham in the final game of the 1985/6 season when they finished second or third and we went down. There was a massive buzz amongst our young firm about the ICF coming to town. We all met up in West Bromwich and made our way down to the Blue Gates - I'd say a good 200 were out, albeit quite young in parts but game enough. We knew what they were about but we really wanted to give it a go. Imagine if we could give a good account of ourselves against the ICF? It would surely get our new firm the reputation we wanted. When we got nearer the ground and feeling up for it, we heard a massive roar from behind and West Ham came running full-pelt up the street. We stood, but the Old Bill got between us and them so some of the young ones, including me as a 20-year-old, were giving it large to the ICF.

Looking at them close up, I thought fuck, they look the real bollocks but I kept thinking there only human like us so fuck them. The police rounded them up and led them into the ground. We did manage to catch a dozen or so of them outside the Brummie Road End and gave them a smacking. During the game we were all saying to meet up under the stand and stick together while psyching each other up. When the whistle went I bounced out of the ground looking for everyone but they'd gone before we all got together. However, it didn't take long to find our firm as they all came running back in with the ICF in hot pursuit. We had obviously been punching way above our weight, but at least we fronted them and put on some sort of show, even though at our young age it was a bit lightweight.

A West Ham lad we knew admitted we were quite plucky but should have stood longer. At that age, I thought that was a good report but a few years later I would have been steaming in. But like so many of the big London clubs we didn't see much of them due to our years in the lower divisions.

Spurs

When I was in my early teens, I remember Spurs coming in our end every year and causing mayhem. Then one year the lads had enough. When they came this particular year in about 1978, there was a big crew of lads from Smethwick waiting for them. Spurs were well up for it, if not a little surprised and we saw Spurs getting escorted round to the away end, they didn't look in the best of shape and I don't remember them going in there again.

Over the years, Spurs became a serious firm. I also remember hundreds of us bumping into them around our back streets by the ground in the 1983/84 season. They were game as fuck but we knocked the fuck out of them, good and proper, with a few Spurs lads seriously hurt. Also the Clubhouse lads took a tasty firm down there in a Cup match in 1983. They had it big time in their seats behind the away fans as someone left the door to that way up open and they steamed in to catch them unawares.

Palace

Total shock this one. Me and my mate were walking through the High Street in West Bromwich one year when we heard a bit of a commotion coming from the side of the Star and Garter pub. To my total surprise there were about 30 Palace lads giving it loads and were coming our way. I shouted "If you want it, follow me" and I took off to our pub at the time, Capers. It was full of our lads and I ran in to tell everyone the good news. Fuck me Palace, never knew what hit them.

We attacked them from all angles and they ran in all directions. The local lads who hung around the games arcade cut them off and I am not joking when I say we ran them for more than two miles before the Old Bill saved them. For a few of them, their day ended in a visit to Sandwell Hospital. We thought they may have wanted revenge, so next time we played them we met in the pub by the train station but they didn't show. We had a large firm out but they did the sensible thing and stayed at home

QPR/Fulham

We've taken large firms to both of these on the train in recent years but again nothing to write about and neither bring firms to us.

Albion skinheads circa 1980s: Snarka, (centre) Keil and Tess

Keil and Snarka

Clubhouse away days, Sunderland 1982: Tats, standing, Bailey looking to his left, Tucker, with back to camera, Tony Malek in denim jacket, Bernie in glasses and Duza looking at camera

Sunderland away continued: Vi, front, a young Bailey and
Clem behind, Big Alfie on left behind lad holding can of
beer and Snarka standing on right at back of coach

Worcester Clubhouse lads at Sunderland away

Blues away – hammer time: L-R Frankie Francis, Joey Clarke, John Payne, Tony Freeth, Gav Pace (in mask) and Harris in Iron Horse pub the day the small firm confronted Blues but received a hammering in the city centre

Young Section 5 Squad patrolling Blackburn in the mid-Eighties.

Lads enjoying Italia 1990 with moustaches on
show - 'Calm down! Calm down!'

PART THREE

Chapter Seven

England Crusades

Tony: While Wolves were bashing the likes of Scarborough and Torquay about, the Section 5 lads were beginning to show up more and more at England games. The first one we took a sizeable firm to was against Scotland in Glasgow in May 1987. There were probably 40 or 50 of us. At this time, you never saw any Dog-heads - Wolves lads - at England games. On this particular trip, we arrived in Scotland's Second City at around 6-ish on the Saturday morning. We'd teamed up with Villa – yes, it still surprises me - but some of our boys from Great Barr, Clem, Peachy and Bailey had become good pals with Gary Little. We went up to the Barrowlands where we were told the pubs opened at 7am. En route we were stopped in our tracks by a couple of Cockney lads who asked who we were. About 30 to 40 yards behind them stood a large firm of around 100, spread all over the street. We said "West Brom and Villa" and the Cockneys looked pretty puzzled as what we'd said spread amongst them. There were blank looks all around from them upon hearing we were together and, much shrugging of shoulders later, we were told that they had no grief with us. But before we walked through them, they asked if we'd seen any Man United. We said we hadn't and it turned out this moody bunch were none other than the ICF and they weren't looking for the Manx for a tot.

We carried on up the road until we finally holed up in a pub called the Eastenders and as everyone got stuck into topping up last night's beers things seemed to be settling down with different firms mixing. Derby, Carlisle, Chelsea, Albion and Villa and many more mingled, trouble-free and talked about the job in hand. Suddenly there was a loud bang outside and as I looked out the window I could see lads running about, total mayhem. I recognised the ICF and they seemed to have found their prey but it all died down very quickly. Apparently, the lads they had attacked with Manc' accents turned out to be Bolton, so the misunderstanding was resolved.

With the beer starting to kick in, the constant singing of the National Anthem and various Loyalist chants were repeatedly belted out. More and more English lads kept arriving we hoped Wolves would make a show, but to be fair we'd never seen any at England games up to then. More importantly, it was a no-show from the Jocks.

So, about noon it was decided to make a move down into a more central area. Hundreds of us marched down to St George's Square in the middle of Glasgow and attacked several pubs full of Scots. I was surprised to see the Jocks didn't really want to play, so a bit of window smashing and jumping around and chanting took place but they didn't want to know. Then, all of a sudden we heard sirens and then van loads of Old Bill came piling through us. The usual manic scenes took place as everything went up but yours truly was by now too pissed to run away so I decided to front the Old Bill. What a mistake that turned out to be. Several coppers headed my way, truncheons drawn. I knew their intentions were not friendly, so I decided I had to make a run for it, fuck knows where. There was total mayhem all around with usual football noise, people running into each other, but I tried to run anyway or so I thought. It turned out I was running on my fucking knees. A big Jock copper with a moustache grappled with me in a flowerbed. I tried in vain to escape, even several mates tried to get me away but they were all over me like a rash. They threw me cuffed-up in the back of their van and another one of our boys, Timmy Bayliss followed.

I made another mistake of continually barracking anything Scottish and more than anything, I kept effin and blinding at my capturer all the way to Stewart Street police station whilst outside sounded like World War III had begun. A bit worse for wear I arrived at the nick, with the big 'tached Jock - who I now knew was called James - glaring at me non-stop. He'd taken a huge dislike to me for my continual rants, especially the ones aimed at him and he refused to take off my cuffs so stupidly I kicked out and spat at him. This time he snapped. He'd had enough and dragged me round a corner and gave me one ferocious kick which landed smack bang in my solar plexus. I thought I'd never catch my breath, the pain was excruciating. He muttered obscenities about my race over and over and I just about got the words "Fuck off" out before he grabbed me by my hair and flung me, pissed, winded and still cuffed-up into the nearest available cell. I felt fucked, everything had caught me up and I drifted into a deep sleep.

When I woke there were two English lads in the cell with me. One turned out to be Villa, the other Newcastle. Little did we know, due to it being a Bank Holiday we were to spend the next three days in that cell. We got on sound, swapping various stories, anything to pass the time. My new pals told me that whilst I was in my coma-like state, that van after van of English lads kept arriving at the station. We were told the total ended up around the 250-mark as England's finest ran amok. A special court was set up for the Tuesday and to my horror, I, along with over 80 other lads was remanded in custody to HMP Barlinnie in Glasgow. Fuck that. It was too late for them to receive prisoners on the Tuesday night, so we had to return the next day. After the normal reception rigmarole, all the English were kept on the same landing.

Obviously the powers-that-be feared trouble from the natives as did we. You can imagine the hostile atmosphere we endured but we just all stuck together. They never let us out into the exercise yard for obvious reasons and all day and night we kept hearing anti-English coursing. We'd just give 'em loads back. I found myself two'd up with a great lad called Mark Gee, who was one of Northampton's main boys. Under the circumstances we had a good laugh. We certainly never felt sorry for ourselves.

Anyway a few days later, I was called out of my cell and told I was to go back to court with about 30 others to see if we qualified for bail. Up there they put you in these tiny rooms, no bigger than the little cells in meat wagons. The locals call them kennels. They take your prison clothes away and bolt the door so you're sitting there in the buff in the dark whilst waiting for them to bring your civvy clothes for court.

I sat there for what seemed a couple of minutes, when the door was half opened. Three other prisoners stood there and one said "You English?" I said yeh and bang! He punched me and then shut the door. It was that quick. The cunt muttered something about fighting in Glasgow before giving me a fucking good right hander which knocked me side ways. I could hear a commotion outside the "kennel" as they kept visiting other English lads. Again, the latch on my door lifted, this time I was ready, quick as a flash I jumped up in a boxer stance - naked.

"What the fuck you doin'?" said the screw standing there with my clothes, in a very agitated Glasgow accent.

"Nothing boss".

"What you done to ya' eye?"

"Nothing boss".

The door slammed shut. Thank fuck for that I thought but I must have looked like a twat. Anyway, I got bailed to return in August when I pleaded guilty to breach of the peace and fined £300. Apparently they had no record of my previous, what a result.

* * * * * * *

Just after Italia 90, England were due to visit Lansdowne Road for a Euro qualifier with Ireland. A crew of around 30 of us travelled via Fishguard due to a drinks ban on the Holyhead route. We met at New Street Station and caught the train to Swansea. Upon arriving in Wales, we had an hour to kill so we dived in the nearest pub. We were in there about 10 minutes when a similar sized mob entered. There were a few sideways glances at each other but no one really bothered. A few of us tried to guess who they were but all we could figure out was that they were Southerners and not very friendly.

We made our way to the waiting train to Fishguard and after settling down in a carriage I set off to the bar for some cans. As I moved down the train I came across a carriage containing the moody Southerners. One little ugly cunt caught my eye as I passed. He looked at me and said in that stupid impression of a Brummie accent that sounds fuck all like it "Where's Bully Bully?" in reference to Steve Bull. "How the fuck do I know? I ain't no Wolves cunt", I said. It was obvious this lot fancied themselves so I did an about turn straight back to our boys. I repeated what had been said which really pissed them off, the cheek of it. We'd never come across any Wolves lads. Then Bailey came back and told us he to had been slagged-off regarding his accent too. After quite a discussion about what needed to be done, it was agreed just to go and front them and explain we are all English and when we arrive in Dublin we'll all be battling on the same side. We made our way to were they were seated, with Peachy leading the way and as the carriage door slid open he punched the first man he saw in the face. What a diplomat. Well, that was it. Cans flew everywhere, one catching me across the eye, lads running over the seats to fight one other, punching, nutting, kicking, screaming, some of them diving for cover. We had them well backed up and after about two minutes of this assault, an elderly guard came running in blowing a whistle, threatening us with the transport police, which stopped everyone in their tracks. The funny thing being, most people sat down opposite or alongside the person they'd been fighting seconds earlier. Everyone shrugged their shoulders and started talking. Some got the weed out and smoked the peace pipe so-to-speak. It turned out we'd just crossed swords with some of Pompey's 657 crew and they had us down as Dog-heads.

When we arrived at Fishgaurd there was a small police presence but nothing was going to happen now. The rest of the trip passed peacefully, although at times you could sense strained relations between the two firms. Nothing much happened except the odd skirmish in Dublin and we drew 1-1. On the way back both firms seemed pretty subdued with some of us drinking together in the bar. We all parted in silence at Bristol but the next time we were to meet, in 1994, it was a lot more volatile.

* * * * * * *

Peachy and Bailey are two lads from the Great Barr area of Birmingham and came through at the end of the Clubhouse era and start of Section 5. They were part of a tight little firm of about 40 lads who hailed from that area as well as West Bromwich, nearby Grits Green and the Yew Tree estate in West Brom. They along with Rich, Heath, (RIP) Burf, his brother John and Jolly, all knocked about together along with Clem who was slightly older, like Bailey, and also well known.

The Great Barr group, nicknamed "The Brummies" by other West Brom lads, would drink in the Scott Arms in Great Barr. It was a pub with a formidable reputation with the likes of Albion, Villa and other firms passing through. Its location, in the middle of a few areas - north of Brum and West Brom and fairly adjacent to Sutton Coldfield - inevitably meant a mixed crowd would drink in there.

Bailey and Clem started to go to matches on the Clubhouse coach after getting to know and mix with Snarka. Bailey first met Snarka at Watford aged about15 or 16 when he and a few others went in their end for the crack and when they inevitably got walked out by the police Snarka noticed them. They were easily the youngest on board at the time, around 1983/4, but were respected lads with the younger ones also looking up to them.

As well as their escapades following Albion, Peachy and Bail' were also regulars on the England scene. Trouble was never far away with Peachy getting arrested on his first trip in Italy in 1990, later in Malaysia, appearing in newspapers after trouble in Stockholm and further adventures in Ireland, Belgium and Holland.

Peachy: Our philosophy wasn't lets smash a pub up, it was if someone turns up to have a row then lets have a row, but we weren't hell-bent on causing trouble, let's just have a good time and that's it. We first went with the travel club in the early Nineties but we got banned eventually so we couldn't get tickets. We got to know some kids from Manchester who could supply us with nicked Inter Rail tickets for about £40 so we could fill them in ourselves which meant free travel across Europe. We'd pack a spare top and jeans maybe, and plan journeys carefully so we could sleep on the overnight services or in the stations and save on hotels and have more beer money. We'd be falling asleep in bars after a crap night's sleep getting on and off the trains and having to show our tickets as we crossed various borders. It was knackering on top of the drinking, fighting, laughing and football and each time we got back we'd be like "I'm not doing that again". But, as the next tournament came round, someone would plant the seed about going then someone else would talk about sorting the Inter Rail option out and so on. The next thing we knew we'd be pissed up and passing out on the floor of a train off to some European destination. We didn't care if there were six or 20 of us it was fine and we knew we'd probably meet up with the same England fans again anyway.

In June 1991, me, Tony Malek, Mark, Glen, Stuart and Bail' and a couple of his mates went to follow England on tour. They played in Australia, a couple of games in New Zealand and a game in Malaysia. It was so humid in Malaysia and we started drinking straight away in the morning. We were absolutely hammered. We were by this outside drinking area, a sort of bar, with plastic chairs and tables and whatever and there was a load of English and Malaysian there and I just lost it. I started throwing things around. I was just drunk and emptied the place within minutes. I went mad, even my mates left me. The bar owner just saw his biggest earning time go. I cleared the patio, everything.

In the ground, it was standing terraces and I fell down them all. I just went gambolling down the lot all the way to the bottom, past everyone and ended up in a crumpled heap at the bottom. All I'd got on was a pair of shorts and in the end I fell asleep face down on the terraces. The next thing I knew, my mates were saying we had to go. I was like "Has the game kicked off yet?" and I was told it had finished. The ground was empty and I didn't know what was going on. My mates said we'd been attacked and had things thrown at us and I couldn't work it out and thought "We're England fans. How did that happen?" The cops took us out onto the pitch and walked us round and out to the main entrance past these Malaysians. I said to people "Get your cameras ready". The Old Bill were around and I steamed into the Malaysians and the cops. About four or five cops dived on me and pinned me down and chucked me into a van. They took me to the police headquarters and I woke up handcuffed to a radiator. Another lad, a Chelsea fan, had been nicked for running onto the pitch nicking the corner flag and attacking the referee with it. He was from Salford I think and that was also his nickname. Well, I thought I'd be alright after hearing what he'd done but they ended up releasing him and told me I'd assaulted a couple of police officers which was worse.

They kept me there, on this chair on the seventh floor of their headquarters for three days. I saw this rat running around but they just said it was an office pet. I remember one copper telling me I was a VIP - a Very Important Prisoner. After three days I was taken to court and I saw all these photographers and film crews outside and thought there must be an important murder case on or something. When they opened the gates, all the media all dived for me - I couldn't believe it - so I got my head down and walked in. In court there were cages which contained about 20 locals but I was given my own. Some prison guard gave me some food, our rations, bundled up in newspaper and I opened it and it was like old rice. I thought no way, the other prisoners all scoffed theirs down but I didn't. One of the locals in another cage, who was probably the only one who could speak a bit of English, just kept shouting "John Major, John Major", at me all the time. I ended up throwing my newspaper food bundle into his cage.

My penalty was a fine or five days in jail and my fine was £200 or something - their highest fine ever as they're usually a couple of quid or something. My travellers' cheques were in the hotel and I had a gold chain round my neck and sovereign rings and when my mates came to see me I took them all off and told them to sell them as fast as possible to get me out. My flight was in two days as well and I had to get the hell out. Luckily they also had a whip round for me and I got out.

The following summer me, Bailey, a lad called Glen from Bewdley who had no idea about footie and just went to games for the laugh went to Stockholm for Euro 1992. It was expensive to drink but we'd go to the outdoors to stock up so we could get tanked up back at the campsite before heading out and having to pay top price for beers. The outdoors were like delicatessens where you took a ticket and had to wait for your number to be served. In one bar, one lad said he'd buy a drink for all the 15 or 20 lads that were out. He had loads of dodgy credit cards on him, all different names and non his, and it took about three or four attempts before one worked. In the first two games we drew with Denmark and France so we needed to beat Sweden to get through. We went 1-0 up but ended up losing 2-1.

We all went to Stockholm for the game and afterwards went marching into the city. The Old Bill were around and obviously lots of lads and people just started looting shops and fighting Stockholm's Black Army and clashing with the cops. We were staying on campsites and police used to dawn raid the tents every morning - it never actually got dark there, it got a bit dusky about 2am then it was light by 4am. The cops would appear most nights or mornings with their torches and drag people out after there'd been trouble. We took the tent down to leave and get train back to Malmo (in Sweden) to head back home. While I was sat on the train, a Swedish guy was sat next to me reading a newspaper and a photo caught my eye and I looked at it and thought "That's me!" It was from the trouble in Stockholm. I remember camera flashes during some trouble and so I just covered my face with my top. Nothing came of it though.

A couple of years later we went to Amsterdam to watch England, possibly in 1994, it was the time when a homemade bomb was thrown. About 10 went over and we expected trouble as the cops were into filming now and it was a bigger scene. As soon as we arrived we went straight to the Red Light area and carried on drinking all day. A few scuffles broke out during the day and as the police presence grew the trouble escalated with bottles flying through the air and a car getting pushed into the canal. The running battles carried on through that area with regular baton charges by the police. One copper on horseback whacked me on my back and I fell to the floor and cut my hand on some broken glass. I darted into a bar, mainly full of supporters watching the trouble. It was then cordoned off by police and they stopped serving. They wouldn't let anyone in or out for about two hours and I knew what was coming. More and more police vans were turning up so I knew we were out of there and going to get deported.

Me and another lad who was injured were taken to hospital for treatment. It was about a 40 minute drive and when we got there it was like a prison hospital. It was deserted. I sat there waiting to get stitched up and when I did I wasn't given any anaesthetic, guess they thought the alcohol I'd had was enough. After that it was back to the police station for interviews. I was told that a copper had been glassed in the face during the trouble and I thought this isn't good as they could assume it was me when I'd genuinely cut my hand on the floor as I fell after being hit. The cell they kept us in was red hot and I'd eaten plenty of kebabs earlier and I was sweating loads and could just smell kebabs. After a bit, the injured copper came into the cell to look at me to see if I was the one who glassed him but he said "Not him". So that was that.

After that we were all taken to the airport and kept in a holding area. We found out that anticipating trouble between England and Holland, the authorities were ready to deport as many fans as possible. Newspapers reported that planes had been chartered to transport home supporters involved in any trouble. It was everyone that had been in the pub so that meant the genuine supporters were getting deported and they were gutted to be flown back to Luton. I still had my match ticket on me and when we landed we all went into the nearest pub – about 30 or 40 of us. But the landlady guessed we'd just got off the plane and what had gone on and wasn't interested in serving us. She told us to go to the next pub so we obliged and ended up watching the game on tv before getting the train home.

About a year later we went for an England v Switzerland friendly. We flew from Luton to Geneva at about 7am and then off to Bern. The flight was delayed which meant the drinking started at the airport. It was mainly full of businessmen when we got on board. We flew over the Alps, enjoyed the view then landed and made our way to Passport Control. There was a line of coppers waiting to greet everyone off the plane and we stood waiting for about 10 minutes before some bloke with a megaphone announced to everyone to bear with them as some were here for the football and others weren't. He said he was going to read some names out and can those identified step forward. He started to read them out and I thought I was alright as mine hadn't cropped up yet but then the last name of the eight he read out was mine. They took us straight to the police cells in the airport and kept us waiting for an hour or two. We got interviewed and I was saying I was just here for the game and that's it but they said I'd been in trouble before and I wasn't welcome. But I was saying "It the European Union. I can go anywhere" But, I later found out Switzerland hasn't ever been part of the EU. We were put back on the same plane.

They had kept it on the tarmac and the eight of us were taken, in handcuffs, to a riot van then to the plane with blue lights flashing. The pilot was asked if he was willing to take us back - with more businessmen, again - and he came into the van and had a look. He said he wouldn't if we were drunk and one lad was all "I've done nothing wrong" so that was him refused but he was alright with the rest of us. The pilot announced to the passengers "These people have been refused entry to the country...sorry for the delay." Obviously businessmen on the plane, which was about 75% full, had no idea what we'd done so were a bit twitchy about us. We still tried to get drinks from the air hostesses even thought it had been made very clear to us there was no way we could indulge once on board and it didn't work. But we were soon back in Luton again and off to the pub. We met about five or six others heading out there and one of them didn't have a ticket so I sold him mine.

None of us had tickets when about crew of about 50 went to Dublin to watch England in the late-Eighties. There were a few locals about and we were by a bar when some Irish bloke asked us how many tickets we wanted. He wanted £100 for each one and told us to come into the bar as I asked to see them. Bailey and another lad hung back a bit but I went in and when he pulled them out, I grabbed them and punched him. They waded in then but he was clinging on to them as much as possible but I managed to grab the stubs and bit of some of the tickets. I managed to get about five or six and everyone was saying we had no chance of using them but at the ground we told officials that someone had tried to snatch them off us which worked and they let us all in.

When Ireland went 1-0 up, the seats started reigning down from the upper tier, where Bailey was, and missiles were flying around. I got up on a fence and unbeknown to me, someone lobbed a bottle of Fanta in my direction. But, luckily someone else jumped up and blocked it, saving me from being knocked off and onto some spiked railings below.

Bailey: When England were playing in Amsterdam in about 2000, a crowd of us flew over from Gatwick. Me and Peachy and everyone had gone through to where you board the plane after Passport Control. I came out of the toilet and saw the cops had got Clem and Peachy and were asking who they were and all that. I spotted a man and a woman going to the plane so I thought I'd walk down with them and I got on okay. Peachy on the other hand was told he couldn't board, although everyone was else was fine. But an announcement was made on the plane "Is there a Mr Bailey on board?" I thought not good, but made myself known and the cops asked if I was with a Mr Peach. I said I was but luckily all they wanted to know was where his bags were. I pointed them out and that was it, off to Amsterdam with Peachy left behind, gutted no doubt.

About 40 of us headed straight to the Red Light area, drinking and eventually Wolves appeared in the bar we were in saying they were looking for Albion. Someone said "There's Gilly!" I didn't even know what he looked like. Then this little fat kid in Burberry popped up in front of us and said "Alright lads. I'm Wolves, you going to run?" He was by the bar and I went for him. The barman had a go at stopping me and the kid ran off with some others but we chased. We ran after them on the street, there were about 25 to 30 Wolves. Gilly did try and stand with another guy but everyone said to get him. We went for him and he was in between some parked cars by a canal. He fell forward and we tried stamping on him but it was hard to get to him. I was shouting "Chuck him in the canal" and I tried but the cops turned up and saved him from an inevitable dunking. I phoned Peachy then and told him I'd chucked his bags off the plane and it's just gone off with Wolves - even more gutting for him.

Peachy: When England played Germany in Belgium in 2000, we were near the ground looking for tickets and I saw a German bloke with one in his shirt pocket and I thought "I'm having that." Bailey was also looking with a couple of lads, a Villa lad and Eamon, when he saw another German guy with one in his hand. He kicked him and snatched it out of his hand. The bloke was with some mates and started shouting but Bail' passed the ticket to his mate and said "Fuck off, what ticket?" showing his empty hands. But Eamon punched the bloke and got arrested.

The ticket Bail got was for the German end and I put my ticket down the front of my trousers. As we walked in a copper said "You've just stolen a ticket." He pulled the ticket out and got on his radio as they had a list of stolen ticket numbers but it had just happened so was too recent to be logged or whatever and we were in. Me and Bail got spilt up but I heard he was pissed up in the German end.

Bailey: I was so hammered during the game I was falling asleep on the German next to me but somehow I found Peachy at half time. Afterwards we thought about our mate that had been arrested and asked where the police station was. We were told to walk into the town centre so we did, for ages and ages...nothing. We saw this female copper and asked her who told us it was about a mile away in the direction we'd just come from. We debated what to do and what was likely to happen to him, trying to justify us going on the piss really and when we decided he'd probably just get deported, and what could we do and all that we hit the bars instead. Back at the campsite the next morning our mate, Eamon, appeared saying so many people had come to see him but not us, his mates from home.

Peachy: For an England qualifier against Poland for 2002 World Cup, the game was in Katowice and we flew to Munich from Birmingham then used the dodgy Inter Rail tickets. We got the sleeper train from Munich to Prague and we slept in the aisles all pissed up and knackered. You'd get woken up on these trips whenever we passed through borders into another country and had to show our passport and tickets. One guard is checking your ticket, another one checks your passports and then again Passport Control checks your passport as you go through different countries. So I'm woken up several times drunk, half asleep and trying to find everything, going through my pockets pulling stuff out and getting mad but sorting it eventually and going back to sleep.

When we arrived, I checked my pockets for everything and got off to go and change some money. I opened my wallet stood in the queue but had absolutely no money in it - the ticket collector must have taken it from my wallet and I was too pissed to notice. We stayed in Prague for a couple of nights then went to Krackow and stayed there for a bit before going on to for the game. In Krackow we went on a tour of Auchswitz, the former German prisoner of war camp. Loads of us went and a few were seig heiling by the gates taking photos and all that but after the tour we were quiet – giving it the biggun' before but after it hit home what had gone on and we shut up. We went back to Krackow and hit the bars in a big square. The plan was for England fans to meet in the John Bull bar and take it from there. There were a lot out drinking and then about 15 or so of us moved on to another club on the other side of the square. There were a few women in there – obviously Catholic - and some lads were dropping their trousers on the dancefloor which wouldn't have gone down well. I was stood at the bar and could see some lads, Poles, coming in. They eventually stopped serving and I could see more and more lads coming in, about 40 or 50 in total. I said to a few that it was going to go off in a bit but most didn't agree and finished drinking up. It was about 20p for a pint so you can imagine we made the most of that. Then the DJ stopped, the bar shut up and the lights came on and we filtered outside. I knew what was coming and outside there were lines and lines of these lads - it was like a tunnel of death. There were about 50 of them and 15 of us, so at least three to every one of us and it kicked off.

We'd run at them and they'd back off but there were more of them behind their front line. They'd grab you and trip you up then another would drag you to the floor and kick you with their Paratrooper boots. It went on for ages, mad battle. You couldn't run off even if you'd wanted to as they were all around. The Old Bill appeared and we thought "Result". But the Poles spoke to them and then the coppers turned round in their cars and left, much to our amazement and fear as well really. We had some good lads but we were outnumbered and we got battered. Some lads got a bad beating and couldn't go to the game later on. I think their feet started hurting with all the kicking and that's how it stopped really.

The next day, the day of the game, lads were bruised, battered and cut. We went to the train station to head off for the match, those that could, and there were about 300-400 lads, all Poles, getting the same train to Katowice. We were like "Not again?!" as we limped up to the station but in the end we decided to get taxis instead. We met more England fans at the game and there were a few scuffles with the locals but there were firms and firms of Poles and they were fighting between themselves too, lots of inter-club rivalries. Inside the ground, England fans were in a little end next to Poles and someone let off a firework or something as players were warming up on the pitch. There was massive bang, no idea where it came from – but it was from the Poles. The players looked up but carried on and it couldn't have put Shearer off as he later scored twice and won it for us. The England fans were trying to get onto the fences to get to the Poles and the riot police waded in. Overall, it was pretty intimidating and opened our eyes to what the Poles were about, which was a bit of a surprise.

* * * * * * *

Snarka: Due to the fact that my marriage of 12 years had come to an unexpected end, I decided to go to the World Cup in Japan in 2002 with two of my mates, Sooty and Karl Malek. They were seasoned England fans who have been following the national side since the Eighties whereas I, on the other hand, had only seen England play at home. But, having got my hands on the tickets for the three group games I set off in the June to the land of the Rising Sun.

Arriving in Tokyo, we quickly got through Customs although a few England fans got pulled over and checked out. By now, I hadn't been involved in football violence for years, neither had my travelling companions. We quickly found our digs for the night which we'd booked on the Internet - one room between the three of us and I had the floor as a "newie" - and off we set in search of somewhere to have a drink. Boy, were we in for a culture shock. We could not find anywhere to drink and never saw another England fan. When we finally found a bar, there was only us in it and the owner had to put the light on for us. We asked him if they were showing the football on his television but he didn't even know there was a World Cup tournament on, his TV was for Karaoke. This happened the next day too. I was starting to think following England wasn't all it was cracked up to be. By the third day, Soot and Karl were ready to fight each other because of the boredom and were seriously talking about going home. I managed to talk them round with the idea of going to the seaside for the day so we found a map and went down to the train station. We pointed out our location on the map to a lady behind the counter and she explained which train to catch and what platform we needed, so off we went. The train was due in seven minutes and as everyone knows, Japanese trains are never late. But as we were waiting for our train, Karl said he needed the toilet, like now. We told him he wouldn't make it back upstairs in time, but he had a brainwave. There was a train on the other platform not due to leave just yet so he went on board for a dump. But as he did so, the train pulled out of the station. We saw him running down the train shouting at the guard to stop it while trying to open the door but to no avail. The train pulled away but Soot said he assumed he'd get off at the next stop and come back to us so we found a bench and waited for his return. Our train came in and went but after waiting for two hours there was still no sign of Karl. We gave up and decided to go back to our digs. As we walked up the stairs the train from the seaside came back with Karl on it. Unbeknown to us, his train had only pulled out to let another one go by. When it reversed into the station he saw the train we were supposed to catch pull up. He ran across to it while Soot and I sat with our back towards him, jumped aboard and went to the seaside, without us. This was to set a pattern with Karl.

England's first match was against Sweden which they drew 1-1. Their next match was with the old enemy, Argentina, and only me and Soot had tickets for this game. We tried to get Karl one but with no luck. The game was to be played in Sapporo, in the north of Japan so it meant an overnight train journey. We hadn't booked the bed on the train so we just tried to get our heads down as best we could. We got drinking Raki with some Japanese and had a great time. We decided to try to sneak into a sleeping compartment and we all managed to find somewhere, albeit all over the train. As the train neared Sapporo the guard came through waking everyone up and as we were waiting for the train to pull in, we realised there was no sign of Karl. We went up and down the train trying to find him and shouting out his name, even the guards were shouting it. We managed to find his bag but there was no sign of him. The train pulled up and everyone got off and by now the guards were going mad. The train was going to be late - something we later found out, that had not happened for 30 years. The train was now four minutes late and me and Soot tried explaining to the guards that he was definitely on the train, somewhere. Just then, Karl popped his head up from a pile of sheets like nothing had happened. We ushered him off as the guards cursed him in Japanese.

We found some digs, dropped our bags off and later on finally found a hotel with a few English fans in and had a good time. The next day we found the fan's party area and saw some Forest fans we'd met in Tokyo when trying to get Karl a ticket. They told us about a Sports bar they had been in the previous night so we arranged to meet them there later that night. We also changed digs as they could only offer us one night in the previous place. As evening neared we set off to find this bar and settled in for the night. It was packed to the rafters with English and Japanese fans and we had a great time. We were squashed right up against the bar and every time the barman turned his back some bottles of Raki were quickly removed by the grabbing hands behind us. He gave us the daggers as he thought it was us who'd nicked his drinks. There were balls, shirts and sports memorabilia being taken off the walls all over the place and all the time he kept looking at us. He even asked us if we have had them and we told him in no uncertain terms that we didn't but he didn't believe us. It was getting late and people were beginning to leave and we decided we'd had enough too and thought about heading back. Karl went to the toilet so me and Soot walked down the stairs to go outside. At the bottom of the stairs we saw that people had discarded their pickings - bottles, shirts, balls and the like - so being drunk and not thinking straight we picked a bottle and a shirt each. I had Jurgen Klinsman's top - God knows why – but as we stepped outside we were confronted by hundreds Japanese police and TV crews. We were immediately surrounded and arrested for theft.

We were handcuffed and shackled and carted off in two separate vans leaving Karl behind. The barman was also arrested for attacking Soot when he came to identify him. As I entered the police station, I was met by a broad Black Country voice saying "You English mate?" I looked up it was our old mate Eamon Payne, a salt of the earth Albion fan who was one of the main lads with the Section 5. "Fuck me. It's Snarka", he said as I was stripped of my clothes and given a grey tracksuit to wear. I was put in a cell with just a blanket and a pillow and settled down for the night. The next morning we were awoken with a breakfast of fish-head soup, needless to say I couldn't eat it. I managed to talk to Eamon through the bars of my cell as he was just two down from me. He told me he and Keiser, his mate from Burnley, had been nicked for using dodgy US dollars and that it didn't look good for him. He said that they only let you out of the cell for 10 minutes for a cigarette break. I have never smoked but when they asked me if I did, I said yes just to get out for a bit. We were ushered to a holding pen were all the local prisoners were sat around a wall. I spotted Eamon and went over and chatted. He told me we could take two fags so I did and sat down by him. I just lit them and held them in my hand. Whenever I tried to speak to Eamon we were told to be quiet, I presume that's what they said as they were speaking in Japanese. After 10 minutes we were put back in our cells and whenever they brought food for us it was inedible soup, like water with bits of floating things in.

I was allowed out of my cell for questioning where I told the interpreter that I was not guilty of anything. He relayed this to the police who just wrote everything down. I was then taken back to my cell and let out for a shower and a soak in a huge tub of hot water. They gave us a wall compartment for a toothbrush and I was then locked up again.

All this time I never once saw Soot but I knew he was in there because although the guards were talking in Japanese, every so often they'd say Arnold Schwarzenegger and Soot's built like him, which made me laugh. I was informed that if we were found guilty we would be sentenced to three months so I had resigned myself to that. That night, England beat Argentina 1-0 but I was stuck in jail. I since found out that Karl had used our ticket and sold the other for a tidy profit. To this day we always rib him about it and say he phoned the Old Bill to get us arrested so he could have our ticket.

The following morning we were finally given something we could actually eat - a giant doughnut and a carton of milk. We found out all the English had been complaining they couldn't eat the food. Later on, a guard came and said in broken English that we had won which if I'm honest didn't really cheer me up as I was stuck in a cell and football seemed irrelevant. A few hours later he came back to my cell and asked me if I wanted a book or magazine. I said yes and was let out to choose one from a pile on the floor. I looked at a few but they were all in Japanese which the guards thought was highly amusing. I declined their offer and went back to my cell. They had also removed my bedding and pillow so I just lay on the floor trying to sleep.

After three nights in jail, I was taken to see the judge. British Embassy officials informed us that we would get three months but, if we pleaded guilty we may just get a fine. So when it was my turn to go before the judge, I was taken into a small room with the judge sitting opposite me and an interpreter alongside me. I said I'd done nothing wrong and had only found the items on the floor. He was more interested in who was in the bar and could not believe we were drinking with Japanese fans. He then said I was being kept in custody for three months where I would then go to a proper court to face the charges. On hearing this I turned to the interpreter and asked if I pleaded guilty what would I get. He asked the judge who said between three months and two years so I decided to plead guilty. I'd been told I would be there for three months anyway so who knows how I would get on at the other court. But the judge said that if I was not guilty I could not therefore plead guilty. I told him I had lied and was ashamed of myself and I had brought shame on my country. I said I never drink and that I was under the influence of alcohol and had abused the Japanese hospitality. I was on a roll now and put my head in my hands as if to show my shame. The judge then spoke to the interpreter for a few minutes, then to me. It must have worked because he said he could tell I was really sorry for what I had done and that as I had learned my lesson I was free to go, with not even a fine.

I couldn't get back to my cell quick enough to be given my clothes to get out. I was met by Soot, Karl and a lady from the British Embassy who confirmed we were free to go with no charges. Karl told us she had been golden and had fought our corner for us. I think they knew we were innocent and were glad there would not be a scene. Soot said he'd the exact same conversation and outcome. All in all, a good result for us but on the down side our mate Eamon spent three months in jail there so big respect to him for being in there that long.

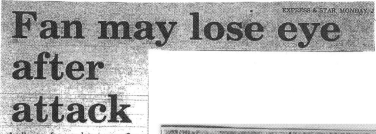

EXPRESS & STAR, MONDAY,

Fan may lose eye after attack

An Everton fan may lose an eye after a minibus full of supporters was ambushed by up to 100 stone-throwing Albion fans branded "wild animals" by shocked police.

Mr Robert McMurray has undergone emergency surgery on his left eye which was injured by shattering glass in the attack.

He was one of seven Everton fans trapped in the minibus as the mob attacked it, bringing terror to a West Bromwich street, after Saturday's cup tie.

Mr McMurray, aged 24, from Liverpool, was today "quite satisfactory" in Sandwell General Hospital.

But it is believed that he has almost certainly lost his sight in the eye, and that he may lose the eye completely.

The hooligans threw a barrage of bricks at the vehicle, smashing all its windows, lobbed lighted paper inside and punched and kicked the terrified occupants.

Helpless

Other horrified Albion supporters, many with children, could only look on helplessly as the gang tried to turn the bus over.

The mob eventually ran from the scene in Roebuck Lane before police arrived, leaving Mr McMurray seriously injured and his shocked friends with cuts and bruises.

Today, Chief Superintendent Keith Pemberton, head of Sandwell police said: "It seems that this mindless minority suddenly turned like a pack of wild animals."

He added: "We hope that all genuine Albion fans will be as appalled as we are at what went on and help us find the culprits," he said.

Hired

The incident happened shortly after 5pm after Saturday's match, which attracted 31,000 and left an estimated further 5,000 unable to get in.

The minibus had been hired by a dozen Everton fans and the seven inside were waiting for their friends before returning to Merseyside.

Detectives at West Bromwich are appealing for witnesses and information on 021 553 2971. Fans can also ring the football watch hotline on 021 550 6177.

Apart from the Roebuck Lane incident, police say there were 15 arrests and six ejections from the ground, but the behaviour of the fans generally was commendable.

Jan 89

Fracas at stadium: British youth fined

By Hew Pit Ling

[text partially illegible]

Fresh being led to the police lockup after the sentencing — NST picture by Shahnaz Sharif

Relegation fans go on the rampage

An injured fan is led away from the Bristol Rovers ground at Bath

West Bromwich Albion fans fought pitched battles and smashed shop windows during a drunken rampage after the club's relegation to the Third Division.

Albion fans ran amok in Bath and Weston-super-Mare after the 1-1 draw with Bristol Rovers.

There were ugly scenes inside Rovers' ground, in Bath, where rival fans clashed during the game on Saturday.

Supporters' club officials later blamed police for failing to keep fans apart.

Drunken

Police also stamped out sporadic outbreaks of trouble at Aston Villa and Walsall.

Ironically, a report published by the Football Trust today paints a picture of improved behaviour on and off the pitch this season, with increasing attendances and rising gate receipts.

In Bath, more than 200 drunken Albion supporters ran riot through the city centre on Saturday night.

At the same time another group of about 40 Albion fans caused more than £12,000 damage after smashing shop windows in Weston-super-Mare's High Street.

Inspector Jack Bradshaw said Bath police made 18 arrests, including 13 Albion fans.

They were all later bailed to appear before magistrates on a variety of public order offences.

At Weston-super-Mare, police battled for nearly four hours to contain rampaging Albion fans.

Police arrested three Albion fans who are still being held.

They face charges of damage, assault and public order offences.

Albion chairman John Silk today claimed the violence was caused by organised troublemakers who had infiltrated the fans.

Mr Roger Homer, chairman of the Albion Supporters' Club, hit out at policing at the match.

At Villa, police made 23 arrests, and three people were slightly hurt during the game against Chelsea.

At Walsall, 12 fans were arrested and 23 thrown out of Bescot Stadium.

● Comment — Page 6.

43-year stadium ban
for football hooligans

Twelve arrested in big game clashes

Twelve people were arrested after clashes between Wolves and West Bromwich Albion fans.

One fan was hit over the head with a bottle and a pub was wrecked near Albion's ground before the Black Country derby on Saturday. Trouble flared before and after the match with 100 fans fighting in West Bromwich High Street and a group of 40 wearing Wolves shirts also rampaged through the Halfway House pub in Old Meeting Street an hour before kick-off.

Bottles and sticks were used to smash up the bar and pub windows causing more than £2,000 damage.

A gang also broke windows at the Waggon and Horses pub, Lewisham Road, near the Hawthorns, before the match.

A 46-year-old man from Newport, Shropshire, who was in Halfords Lane with his wife just before kick off, suffered a cut head after being hit with a bottle.

Albion fans threw coins at Watson fans in the ground and there was also a fight at Junction 1 of the M5 between gangs after the match.

Chief Supt George Dunwoody, head of Sandwell police, said: "It is unacceptable that this should happen at a football match when the majority of people come along to watch a game.

"There were problems with four cars being vandalised and that attack on an innocent fan which worried me."

He said that out of the 12 arrests for affray, disorder and drunk and disorderly conduct, six people had been cautioned and are charged to appear at West Bromwich magistrates court in February.

Dennis Turner, Labour MP for Wolverhampton South East, also president of Bilston Town FC, said: "I think the whole episode is inexcusable.

These mindless thugs should be dealt with severely by the football authorities and the police.

"They bring the name of Wolverhampton into disrepute.

Watson club secretary Tony Foss also condemned the hooligans.

"If anyone is convicted of violence at Molineux their season ticket is taken away and they are banned," he said.

"When the people responsible for the weekend's violence are identified, we will take very strong action."

Gangs on rampage as hardcore 100 plot violence
SOCCER THUGS' APPOINTMENT WITH TERROR

By Wat Matthews

SOCCER thugs armed with CS and pepper sprays, bricks and bottles clashed in Wolverhampton as pre-arranged violence erupted in the town centre.

They fought and hurled missiles at each other before and after the derby match between Wolves and West Bromwich Albion.

Dog handlers, mounted police and scores of officers armed with batons were drafted in to tackle the crowds as the fans behaviour spilled overboard.

Police under-condemned the thugs as "animals" and said violence was organised by about 100 troublemakers.

Scores of people went before or beyond and after about 20 arrests before and after Saturday's match, which Wolves lost 1-0.

Several people went before the police dogs as officers tried to maintain order and keep in hooligans as he tried to restrain gangs of a fan and another policeman was wounded in Chapel Ash.

Magistrates heard that a Wolves fan had been escorted by police to prison with his hands tied in New Cross Hospital.

He said the violence was orchestrated by about 100 thugs. Police used pepper sprays and the fans charged down to watch their rival gangs.

"We would see town hooligans working in small trouble spots, moving on to try it on the pub. It may have been fear money," he added.

But he emphasised that there was a few people at the event itself.

DISCUSS

Chief Inspector Tom Stuffer asked that police should be meeting with local police and scoured and other bodies to discuss measures to prevent similar trouble.

He said they would like a camera system, watching the timing of fixtures when the possibility of getting such a number technology.

"Scenes as fans fought running battles along the narrow and undermanned 24 hour town centre world.

"There were numbers of uniform worried by road crowds of rowdy supporters intent on causing trouble, said Inspector Stuffer later.

"They were fighting, throwing missiles and other people saw CS spray as well as batons and police officers.

"Nothing broke out of Preston Street and its monster before kick-off when groups of fans came together at each other battles and broke at each other.

Terrified shoppers and inside shops and many shopkeepers locked their doors as not up security measures.

PC Paul Shaffer of British Transport Police said a special team – complete with a police escort – was ordered to drive Albion fans out of Wolver-

Police escort fans down Tower Street after the late ...

Jan 2000

POLICE BATON CHARGE ON FEUDING FANS

By Susan Leigh

POLICE officers were forced to baton charge two groups of football supporters to stop a clash between rival Albion and Wolves fans after the Black Country derby at Molineux.

The officers had to take action when Albion supporters stopped to confront a large crowd of Wolves fans at the bottom of Camp Street between Molineux Street and Stafford Road.

The incident happened just after the final whistle blew signalling Wolves 3-1 victory over Albion.

A total of 41 fans were arrested during and after the match incident.

Police said there resulted could have got wrapped under control during action.

A Broms-road man from Smethwick was a 24-year-old member Broths-rev both arrested on suspicion of public worders of assault and breach proving further injuries.

Five Albion supporters were all arrested on suspicion a breach of the peace but no further action was taken against them. They were a 34-year-old man from Smethwick, a 39-year-old from Wotton Green, a 35-year-old man from Wyson Green, a 33-year-old man from Oldbury and a 34-year-old man from Bearwood.

RECOGNISE

A 25 year old man from Brown Regis a 31-year-old Tipton man and a 40 year old man from Bloxwich were all arrested and charged with public order offences and later bailed to appear at Wolverhampton magistrates court on March 22.

Superintendent John Watson of Wolverhampton police said: "We used every resource that they could bring under control."

Running battle as rival soccer fans clash

More than 100 rival Wolves and West....Bromwich Albion fans were involved in a running battle after clashing outside a Coseley pub.

Two were treated at hospital for minor injuries.

Another two were arrested and charged with public order offences.

The fight followed yesterday's Black Country derby between the two rival First Division clubs at Molineux.

Wolverhampton police had praised the performance of the two sets of fans following the 1-1 draw.

But two hours after the final whistle, more than 100 of them on their way home to the Dudley area met head-on outside the Royal pub in Castle Street, Coseley.

Chief Inspector Mick Jones, of Dudley police, said the disturbance started with about 30 fans involved and escalated as police tried to separate them.

A window in the pub was smashed and it took police about half an hour to bring the opposing factions under control.

But Insp David Whatton, of Wolverhampton Police, said he had been pleasantly surprised by the good behaviour of most of the 26,000 Molineux crowd.

"We had a high number of officers at the match but we were able to return to normal levels of policing at night and there was next to no trouble in town," he said

aug 93

● Savage fans 'shocking and disgusting'
● Police ban Wolves-Albion night clashes

Derby violence the worst ever

By Dave Lawley

A POLICE chief today hit out at Albion and Wolves fans for "the worst acts of violence" he had experienced at a football match.

Chief Superintendent Bruce Gilbert, who was in charge of last night's game at the Hawthorns, said as a result they would now refuse to allow any night games between the two rival clubs.

Mr Gilbert said the total of 41 fights between the fans was unbelievable. He said: "There was a hardcore of serious boot-boys from both sides who were just out for trouble."

The hardcore police chief was worn than 200 officers were involved in the night, a number they had been expected to cut back.

There were only four arrests but the battle could have been much higher as officers cannot step in, wishing and watching the crowds.

He said: "I can asre Wolves fans travelled down the green towards the Hawthorns end.

"Albion were out there made but they erupted this were looking for the Albion factions along with waiting for a goal.

"It was all shouting and pushing," he said.

Oct 2001

Hooligans trash pub during violent football derby-day fight

'Fans' exposed as HOOLIGANS

---

day, May 27, 2005

Four supporters plead guilty but 18 deny violence charges

Albion fans in court over derby day fight

By Jim Dunton

Four West Bromwich Albion fans have admitted their part in a brawl after a Premiership derby with Aston Villa.

A total of 22 fans of the club appeared before a judge at Birmingham Crown Court yesterday. They were charged with violent disorder over the August 22 clash involving up to 80 people. The incident, near the Uplands pub in Oxhill Road, Handsworth, was a pre-arranged fight, police have alleged.

FOOTBALL THUGS RUN RIOT

Hooligans clash after Albion-Villa derby

SCORES of football hooligans armed with baseball bats and iron bars fought pitched battles with riot police after going on a terrifying rampage following the Albion-Villa derby.

Eight fans were injured and 12 arrested as up to 80 people confronted each other in what police said was prearranged violence two hours after the final whistle yesterday.

Residents today spoke of the terrifying ordeal as the battle raged.

● FULL STORY: PAGE 2

Net is closing on Albion soccer thugs

By Russell Youll

Fighting fans in Albion rumpus

Two-goal Lee saves a point

...bion's First Division ...tch with Bristol City ...s held up for 13 ...nutes by fighting fans ...he Smethwick End at ...Hawthorns.

Bail football ban for accused fan

City fan admits violence

Albion bans 13 yobs from home games

Thirteen fans have been banned from Albion matches indefinitely after being arrested for public order offences following clashes ahead of the club's game against Cardiff, it emerged today.

The supporters, six of whom are season ticket holders, were initially charged with affray in the wake of an incident in Birmingham Road, near Junction 1 of the M5.

The charges were later reduced to threatening behaviour and conduct likely to cause a breach of the peace, of which they were found guilty. All 13 were given conditional discharges and various fines by magistrates – but not banning orders as West Midlands Police had hoped.

But Albion officials have now exercised their own right to exclude them from The Hawthorns, claiming it is in the best interests of the club. The Baggies have now sent letters out informing the fans of their decision and will refuse to sell them tickets for both home and away matches.

The club will also recommend they are banned from any ground Albion play at, if necessary. Secretary director Dr John Evans said: "We hope our fans, the vast majority of whom are well behaved, will recognise this action as underlining the seriousness with which we regard these offences. Football is almost always about rivalry but it should never be about violence."

Dr Evans stressed the decision was not a reflection of what had happened ...

...2 BRISTOL CITY 2

...ios at The Hawthorns

...scored a dramatic last-minute ...h a point for Albion.

...s had looked down and out after ...fired Bristol 2-1 ahead with just ...to go.

...as spoiled by fighting between ...sides, which delayed the start of ...half by 13 minutes.

...ERLAND 2 WOLVES 1

...ans held ...n swoops

...ven West Bromwich ...n fans were being questioned today after being ...ted in dawn raids.

...e men – aged between ...d 35 – were arrested as ...ected football hooligans ...art of a nationwide ...down.

...ey were targeted after ...g spotted on film evidence obtained during hooli... ...problems at the recent ...n-Cardiff City match ... men from Kiddermin... Cradley Heath, Rowley ... Darlaston, Tipton, ...sbury and West ...wich were being questioned today. The police want ...g orders on them.

● Suspects – Page 7

FANS IN COURT AFTER BRAWL ON SEAFRONT

By Emma Kilvert and Sunita Patel

A WEST Bromwich Albion fan ... a Wolves supporter appeared ... court today in connection with ... weekend brawl in Blackpool.

More than 200 fans, followers of Wolves, ... and Birmingham City, are alleged to have ... involved in incidents after converging on ... seaside town's promenade on Saturday.

One man is in hospital with stab wounds.

ARRESTS

Public forc... to flee from the violenc...

Clash... follow... big lo...

Guests

Train stat... with no d...

Arrests over Baggies fans rampa

SWOOPS IN
YOBS HUN

By Dan Slee

POLICE today arrested five suspected hooligans in connection with rioting by West Bromwich Albion fans.

The trouble in West Bromwich High Street followed the promotion clinching game against Crystal Palace on April 21. All of those arrested have been served with banning orders which stop them travelling to the World Cup and attending other football matches.

Officers dressed in plain-clothes were swooped on addresses in West Bromwich, Hilston, Tividale and Smethwick at 6 o'clock this morning to arrest three of the men.

Two others were detained later in the morning as part of Operation Navalis.

All five were taken to Wednesbury police station where they were served with the banning orders and charged with violent disorder.

...were stopped... broke out in West Bromwich the... Baggies riot. One gang... Police...

...ority

Chief Inspector... ...man, who is said, "All have been identified as offenders, with violent disorder, owing to considerable that type... it can be said... the first phase... tion and we are... er arrests. ...your appeal f... two individuals... ...uals connected order to quote...

...made in High... and officers attacked by four prompts... be deployed an inside

---

Street clashes as police face partying fans

By Ken Tudor

Squads of police in riot gear sealed off parts of West Bromwich as the celebrations of Albion's promotion victory turned sour.

Within half an hour scenes of happy Baggies fans dancing in the street yesterday evening were replaced by violent clashes between police and groups of supporters.

About 10 people were arrested at the end of a bitter sweet day for the Black Country. Shocked and bewildered fans, some of them bleeding from alleged baton blows, claimed that the police had over-reacted to the jubilant scenes on the street.

But police said they had responded to reports of drunken fans jumping on cars and attempts to try to tip some of them over. They said that people had complained that they were in danger because of the behaviour of fans.

Helicopter

Columns of riot police pushed their way up the High Street from near the West Bromwich Building Society offices for about 20 minutes until the crowd of people, many protesting about the police action, finally dispersed.

Fan Warren Walker, of Greets Green, accused police of a too tough response to the scenes in High Street. "It was a total over-reaction," he said. "We had batons, shields and a flaming helicopter over us. It was like something out of a film."

John Humphreys, of Black Lake, said the whole atmosphere turned in a few minutes. "There was a lot of pushing on the street but the police turned really heavy-handed. Sadly this encouraged the louts to throw bottles and then it just escalated. What a shame - it had been a great day until then," he said.

Soccer fans riot angers police

POLICE are to complain to the Football League after officers in riot gear were forced into battle at Sheffield Midland station to separate rival fans in what was described as "mob violence".

One policeman was injured in clashes with West Brom fans and officers were forced to use batons to deal with fighting between Birmingham and West Brom supporters on Saturday.

But police are angry that fixtures had been organised to bring two rival sets of fans together in South Yorkshire.

Supt Martin Hemingway, of South Yorkshire Police, said: "What were people thinking of?

"To organise two fixtures like this so that two sets of rival fans are forced to use the same railway station at the same time it seems incredible.

"We will be in contact with the Football League about this. It was the worst football violence this season."

The fans had been on their way home from separate clashes in the county - Birmingham at Sheffield United at Bramall Lane, and West Brom at Rotherham.

Police had been on high alert as the United match as the two sets of supporters have a history of

By Tony Belshaw

hostility towards each other. Hooligan gangs associated with both teams - United's Blades Business Crew and City's Zulus - have clashed in the past.

The match passed off peacefully.

But trouble later flared in The Cossack pub in Sheffield city centre when Birmingham fans became increasingly boisterous.

They were led to the station by police to await their train - when Albion fans arrived from Rotherham to wait for the same train back to the West Midlands.

"The West Brom fans were displaying extreme violence towards officers. Around 30 officers were forced to use batons to beat Hemingway," said Supt Hemingway.

Horrified

"The officers demonstrated a resilience in protecting the general public, who were quite horrified by what they saw."

In Doncaster several arrests were made when fans started fighting in Yates' Wine Lodge in Cleveland Street before the Doncaster Rovers v Scunthorpe United match.

A man from the West Midlands, who has not been named, was charged with violent disorder. He was bailed to attend Doncaster Magistrates on December 8.

Three other people were arrested and cautioned.

PART FOUR

Chapter Eight
Toffees, Trotters n' Jail Terms

Tony: Back in England our ever-growing firm was going from strength to strength, surprising firms both home and away. There were battles with Man City, Forest, Plymouth, Reading and Barnsley, after which the Payne brothers - Johnny and Eamon - and several others were jailed for affray. We were a very confident and more established firm by now so when we drew Everton in the third round of the F.A cup in 1989 we couldn't wait to try our luck with some Scousers as they were top of Division One at the time.

Everyman and his dog was out for this one and on the way to the Hawthorns, I'd say we'd mustered a firm of around 200. Word got back that a crew of Everton were in the Three Mile Oak, up by the M5 motorway island. We didn't waste much time landing outside it. A few Scousers were outside and rushed inside to close the doors. We put a few windows in, but they just wouldn't come out. The police arrived pretty quickly and moved us on towards the ground. Being banned, me and few others headed back into West Brom for a beer and as the final whistle went we were outside the ground to meet the rest of our firm. We walked back to the Three Mile Oak as we thought the Scousers would be around there. Sure enough in the street at the side of the pub was a couple or three minibuses parked up. As I opened the door and enquired as to whom they were, I was met with a good dig in the mouth from the driver. They steamed out of the van giving it loads. Trouble was they couldn't see that there were loads of us lurking in the dark. P, one of my pals from the Stone Cross area snatched the keys and all hell broke loose. The Scousers ran back inside the van for cover and the ones that couldn't took terrible hidings. One or two managed to escape but a horrific attack took place on the remaining Evertonians.

Every single bit of that van was smashed to smithereens and the occupants repeatedly beaten with bricks, sticks, fists, boots, bits of glass and tools for at least five, very long minutes. Some lads tried to set fire to the van and overturn it. By anyone's standards it really was a horrendous and vicious attack. Eventually the baying crowd dispersed as sirens filled the night air, but for one poor lad it was too late to save the sight of his one eye. Some of the injuries sustained were quite gruesome and for the next week it was all over the local news as well as the national press. Interviews with the police were shown on the local news with pictures of the injured lad and pictures of the van which had to be scrapped. The police were saying they "would not rest until they had found those responsible".

Sure enough, true to their word on Friday 13 January 1989, 43 suspects were arrested after dawn raids in Birmingham and the Black Country as part of Operation Scouse. I wasn't nicked straight away as I hadn't stayed at home the night before and knew nothing about it until someone working on the building site with me showed me the lunchtime edition of the Evening Mail newspaper. No sooner had I'd found out about it, I was arrested by two plain clothes officers on suspicion of Section 18 wounding with intent and affray. After hours of questioning we were locked up overnight to appear before a special sitting at the West Brom courts on the Saturday morning. Bail wasn't given to the 14 lads who were finally charged with the attack. After two weeks on remanded in Winson Green in Birmingham due to the kindness of two friends who put up some cash I was at last given conditional bail. The police continually hounded me for the following months checking that I was in the house most Saturdays from 10am to 6pm.

A week before the trial we had some good news as the Section 18 wounding charge was dropped, only right too as I know for a fact none of us did the lad's eye. The police said the injury was caused by a brick and as the lad was wearing glasses his retina was cut. Bricks and the like were thrown but not by me nor anyone else in close proximity to the van as there was no need. The trial was set for 5 May later the same year and we had all been advised to plead guilty. As the day progressed, things looked grim because during the summing up the judge told all 13 of us – one lad had to walk - that it wasn't a case of if we go to prison but, how long the custodial sentences would be. Toby and I got the longest sentences with 18 months each which, considering my brief had said three years was a good result. We also got two-year bans from football. After our release from jail in Stafford in the December, I discovered not a lot was happening at the football due to the rave scene taking over. Football lads everywhere were getting too fucked up on ecstasy each week to bother getting out of bed Saturdays let alone rowing up matches.

The replay was scheduled a few days later and it was clear and perhaps inevitable Everton wanted revenge. In Andy Nicholls's book, Scally, he talks about "an eye for an eye" and how he carried out vicious attack on a West Brom lad.

He wrote that after the game, the lad, wearing a bib and brace and a silver baseball cap, was holding his hands over his face as he lay on the floor fending off Nicholls's frenzied slashing and vicious attempts to get to his eye. The strength of the lad prevented that from happening but his fingers were "cut to the bone" and his screams put an end to the attack as the noise prompted the curtains on nearby houses to start twitching.

However, there is genuine confusion amongst the West Brom firm about who the victim was. The severity of the incident he talks about would surely mean word would spread rapidly with the lad no doubt needing extensive hospital treatment but no one heard of such a serious incident taking place. It has led several to believe that it relates to a minor incident before the game between about 30 Everton lads and about eight from West Brom. One lad was slashed but his wax jacket took the brunt of it and his nose was broken after being hit in the face by a blunt instrument. As this is the story the lads believe Nicholls was referring to they maintain he has exaggerated it somewhat for whatever reason. The lad, who wishes to remain nameless, picks up the story:

We were about 18 or 19 at the time and there was just a few of us walking on our way to the ground. We asked someone where the away end was but they pointed us in the wrong direction and we ended up near the home end so we had to go all the way back round and by the time we'd walked round we realised we were being followed by about 30 lads. We got back onto the main road, there were about eight of us in total and we were heading back towards the away end again. We could hear these lads getting closer and I turned around and as I did I got hit full on the nose by some blunt instrument, definitely not a punch, which later I found out had broken my nose.

My instinct then was to lash out at the nearest person to me and I had a little scuffle with a lad who I traded blows with, with not much resistance. There was a bit of fighting going on and they were around us then. I just ran at one lad on the end of their mob to try to get through them and threw a punch, don't even know if it connected properly, but I got past them and back up towards the away end where the police intervened and prevented further trouble. We were then led to the away end and we started queuing to get into the game when one of my mates noticed that the back of my coat was cut. On further inspection I found out that it had gone through my T-shirt and I had a six-inch cut but it didn't require stitches. If the game had been in the summer instead of a cold January evening I am sure my back would have required a few dozen stitches.

After the game, we all walked back to the cars amongst a massive Albion following and nothing happened. The clothing he (Nicholls) talks about in his book was nothing like what I was wearing but we never heard about anyone getting attacked like that, so it must be me? I was slashed and my nose was broken and it sounds like a vicious attack so we think it's me he is talking about, but, it was hardly like the frenzied attack he described. In fact, I was well enough to visit Watford three days later. But, against what he said, he has totally elaborated and overblown but I suppose it helped him sell his book.

* * * * * * *

Another memorable battle which resulted in a spell in prison for a few lads was after a trip to Bolton in 1991. Peachy tells the story:

It was a hot, sunny day when we played Bolton in September 1991 and about 60 of us went up on the train to Manchester where we met some Bolton lads that we knew from the England scene. We had a few beers there then walked to Victoria then off to Bolton. We thought we'd have a night out in Blackpool afterwards as well. The lads told us to watch out for the CCTV cameras that had been put up. It wasn't such a big thing then, so we thought yeh whatever, okay.

We saw Pc Carling there, our football intelligence officer, who always used to give me a hard time. They were there filming us which is par for the course really. Anyway, we went to the ground and we got beat 3-0 or 3-1 or something. Afterwards, we came out and started walking to the town centre. We met a few more who had made their own way up there too. Those on coaches and trains had gone. About 100 of us walked into town and the first pub we got to, everyone was stood outside as it was such a hot, sunny day. They were looking at us as we approached then the glasses came raining down on us. We steamed into them and they got on their toes and ran off to the next pub. We went to the next pub and there was about 50 more lads there, about 120-odd of them again in total. They came out throwing glasses and bottles and we were saying just keep walking at them, just keep walking. We got to them, straight in. A milk bottle came flying over by me and landed right by my foot with the neck facing down with the head snapped off. I picked it up and threw it back and we chased them again and then the police came.

We went to next pub, they came at us, we went into them, stood for a bit but, basically it was us running them through their own town. The police came again so we dropped the shoulder and did one and got the train out to Manchester. We met up with two of the Bolton lads from earlier and they came back to Manchester with us. We went to a place called Shambles Square and Man United had been playing at home and there were about 300 of them in the square. There were about 40-odd of us now, we'd whittled down a bit. We had a drink and they were aware of us, everyone was outside looking at us. We had a couple of beers before going to Piccadilly to get the train to go to Blackpool. We walked through square and it is different now but then it was enclosed and there was just a walkway to get in or out. Anyway, these two Bolton fans started singing "Who's that dying on the runway?", and we joined in. We got chased out of the square and just as we went out through the walkway about 100 pint glasses came our way and luckily hit the wall or roof bit we were going under. We did a left up the road into the city centre and we'd run about 100 yards with them behind us. We'd run, they chased, then a few of theirs dropped off, we'd stop get our breath, then carry on and a few more of them would drop off and so on. But after a bit, I said "Right then, stop running now", so we did and turned around. There were about 40 of them now and we ran straight into them. It went off and we gave them a right kicking. The Old Bill turned up and Man United were allowed to walk away and all of us got nicked - well, about 20 of us were as few others drifted off and escaped when cops showed up.

We were taken to the central lock up in Manchester, kept till Monday morning then up in court charged with violent disorder. We got bail and the case kept getting adjourned until it eventually went to Crown. One of the days we turned up at court our solicitor said a certain number of us were going to get re-arrested. The judge said all on bail apart from...and the names were read out including mine, about eight of us in total. We were re-arrested, put in cells and the police van and driven back to Bolton. We were interviewed by police at Bolton police station and it was all about the time when we first got off the train when they were filming us in Bolton. One at a time we were interviewed and they showed us pictures and stills of us from throughout the day and all of said "No comment". We'd all been chatting between the cells saying we thought we're banged to rights. I was the last one in and they were like "Would you say this is a good likeness to yourself...?" "No comment." I knew what was coming and out came the CCTV and they showed us that too. I got charged with violent disorder again despite our no comments. We got bail and the others that didn't get arrested had come over to Bolton and were in the pub down the road waiting as we came out one by one. The police asked if I had anything to say before I was bailed and given my property back. I said "No. "No reply" to which they replied "Makes a change from no comment".

So we were back up to court every so often then it went to trial with the Manchester incident first. All they had against us was one bystander stood in the dock. He was asked what did he see etc. He said he saw West Brom supporters. When were asked how he knew they were West Brom, he said it was because he'd been told. He got the story so wrong. We found out later it was some sort of homeless alcoholic or something and our barrister had a good go at him and pulled it apart. The whole case was thrown out against everyone. One down. One to go.

So for the Bolton one it was the CCTV evidence. In early Nineties the pictures weren't that clear. We had copies and they were shit. But, in court it was a lot clearer and three out of the nine of us in court were convicted, including me, Rich and Bladesy. I got one month in jail, Rich got 240-hours Community Service and Bladesy got three months.

Cola, a well known lad who started going in the mid-Eighties, was also involved in the trouble at Bolton.

After the game, it went off big style. The Old Bill got us on CCTV and that would have been discarded was it not for what happened in Manchester later. It was alright until it all went off. There were about 100 after us and we'd run, then a few of theirs would drop off to about 80 then about 40. We got to top of the hill and it was comical. There were about 20 of them by now and about 15 of us and we were ahead of them but needed to catch our breath and so did they. So we stopped and were like "Hang on a bit", and had our hands on our knees, panting. They were doing the same and saying "Yeh, fine", as we'd all run so much. It was funny and eventually we stood and fought them.

The Old Bill came and people did what they could to disappear but got rounded up. We couldn't get bail but there were riots on at Strangeways at the time so we got put in different police stations instead to wait for court on the Monday. Then the cops wanted to know why we were in Manchester and they realised we'd played Bolton earlier on. So they asked Bolton police if there had been any trouble there and they said yeh too right so they got the CCTV footage for that which led to more arrests. In court the judge said Bolton was the "first part of the day of destruction".

I was acquitted, as were a few, as there were problems with getting witnesses."

Chapter Nine

No Life in the Third Division

Tony: It was the early Nineties and lads seemed to be going back to the footy. Albion were now deep in relegation trouble, staring at going down to the third tier of English football for the first time in our history. As always seems to be the case, it went down to our last game in 1991, away to Bristol Rovers, who at the time were playing at Twerton Park in Bath. It was also my first League game since the Everton ban, by just two days.

About 100 of us met up West Brom early doors and made our way down the M5 to Weston-super-Mare. The plan was to ditch the vans and cars there and jump on British Rail to Bristol/Bath. As the day progressed more and more of our boys came down and joined in the crack around the various pubs we'd taken over. It turned into a right Beano (mad one). As we made our way to the station I remember thinking we had one of those untouchable firms out. I suppose every firm has days like that. Anyway, we were having a right laugh fucking about on the train. I was standing in the buffet bar buying a few cans when all these blokes got on at Bristol. They looked well up for it and came straight onto this pokey little buffet bar that contained me and one other lad. On hearing me order my cans, they decided to take the piss about us going down, as well as my accent. I waited for the train to pull away and I made my way - with howls of laughter going on over my shoulder - to my comrades at the other end of the train. I told them what had gone on and it was off. We steamed through the train until we got to the buffet bar. I still remember the look of "Oh fuck" on their faces but it was too late to go anywhere as we barged our

92

way in and battered all we came across. "Not so fucking game now are ya?" as we repaid these Bristol boys for their stupidity. They got kicked, punched, pulled and nutted from all angles and one of our lads had taken a walking stick off Big Boris who had a broken ankle, and repeatedly whacked them about the head with it. They were in bits as lads stomped them into the floor. As the train came to an abrupt halt, police piled on and into most of the carriages. I sneaked off the train just as I heard Big Boris pleading his innocence to the Old Bill. Apparently one of the Rovers boys had identified him as the culprit who'd been smacking them about with his walking stick. Poor sod I thought as I saw them lead him away.

I followed the fans and made my way to Twerton Park where I could see Albion fans all over trying to get tickets. To my knowledge only a small percentage of our crew had them. I tried various turnstiles, home/away, trying to blag my way in. They must have been the most honest turnstile operators in the country. I just couldn't get in. There had apparently been plenty of trouble in and around the ground already and operators had been told to be vigilant. I made my way round to the end where the Albion supporters were supposed to be, they'd only given us around 1,200 tickets. Just before I got there I spotted a steward walking down some steps from what looked like a couple of porta-cabins on top of one another. I thought I'd try my luck so I just casually walked up the stairs which led to a kind of balcony. I parked my arse right there with another one of our boys, Glenn, and thought if we get caught, we get caught. After about 15 minutes, just as we were thinking it was our lucky day as no one had bothered us, a door opened and there stood a very shocked-looking middle-aged man dressed in a club tie and blazer. We met him with kind smiles and apologies, offering handshakes and sob stories about our lost tickets and it seemed to work. He turned out to be none other than the Bristol Rovers secretary.

After his initial shock of us being there, we told him we were good law abiding Baggies fans and after endless yarns about our two clubs he said we could stay but only for the rest of the half as he would have to leave. When half time arrived, we obviously thought that was that but he turned to us and asked "Are you two hooligans?" Certainly not we replied and he hesitated for a second then beckoned for us to follow him. To our astonishment he called a steward over and told him to open the gate and let his two "friends" in and after a few good lucks and handshakes we were in.

During the second half, every now and then you would hear roars and sirens and towards the end of the game a few boys appeared on the home end roof. Apparently our firm had been bang at it with the local police during the game and some had even paid locals to view the game from their back gardens which overlooked Twerton Park. But as the final whistle went the unthinkable had happened, the 1-1 draw just wasn't enough, we were down! It was a sad firm that got together afterwards but, it was one looking for revenge due to our relegation. So, Rovers had to pay for it and by fuck they did. We were going mental as we steamed towards the train station. We were met by groups of their lads who took some ferocious beatings. Game as they were, we were in no mood to fuck about. The police were in danger of losing control. I saw one lad get run over as cars sped to get out of the way of the rioting Albion lads. Re-enforcements in the shape of mounted police slowly restored order and escorted us back to our train. But they got the right hump as they thought we'd be getting the train back to Birmingham and after long arguments they realised they had no choice but to let us back into Weston as all our transport and B&B's were there.

Once back in Weston, things escalated as hundreds of drunken Albion lads basically wrecked the place, smashing up pubs having running battles with police and locals. It was total carnage. I saw a motorbike put through a shop window, properties were broken into and locals were taxed along with fighting in nightclubs. Quite a few of our lads got lifted as the trouble went on most of the night and into the early hours.

In the morning when we went looking for a café, Weston looked more like Beirut. Since then, I've seen Albion fans in shirts in Weston getting filthy glares from the locals. We eventually made our way back to West Brom, tired and gutted as the reality of what had happened sunk in. I remember one of the lads in the van saying there were some "game" firms in the Third. Scant compensation I thought but, bring 'em fucking on.

* * * * * * *

As the new season progressed, if there were loads of good firms we didn't come across many, except for the obvious, Blues and Stoke. They were obviously big games for us. On the morning of the Stoke game we met up in the Star and Garter - our HQ in West Brom - then travelled in cars. We parked up and about 20 of us made our way towards the ground. On the way we came across a pub called the Glebe. As we approached it, a Stoke fan stood at the door said we were okay for a drink so we walked through the bar into the lounge. I turned to my mate Wilf, a very game lad on the scene at the time, and asked him if he'd clocked the lad sitting in the corner of the bar. He said he hadn't but I saw the lad nearly choke on his pint when we walked in and off he went. Didn't need a rocket scientist to work out where he was going. We went in the lounge where there was a mix of fans. We started to order the beers when that familiar roar went up. Stoke were in the doorway unloading glasses and bottles at us. JL got a glass straight across the eyebrow which had to be stitched and a few shirters copped it too. We had nowhere to go but back at them so we hurled stools, tables, ashtrays and the like and to my amazement they trapped but in doing so got stuck in the doorway and took a bit of a pasting as we piled into them. All of a sudden, there was lots of shouting by the men in blue as the pub quickly became full of police. We heard they'd had some sort of warning about us being in the pub and steamed through the bar into the lounge via the counter. The police were going mental and exchanged angry words with the gaffer. They then drove us out of the pub and into the ground but fair-play to Stoke for the invite however, that was that for the day.

Whilst down in the Third Division it was always us, Stoke and Blues up at the top which led to a few minor scuffles between us and them but nothing to really write home about, as you can imagine. Although all the firms had big turn-outs for the games, our Old Bill seemed to be in control by managing to head off anything too serious. On the pitch, our first season ended up in disappointment by finishing seventh, despite a 5-0 win at Shrewsbury at the last game of the season. The match ended up with several pitch invasions, scuffles in the crowd and the crossbars getting snapped by Albion lads, which Phil E from Handsworth describes next. It was also the last time Bobby Gould was in charge, with Ossie Ardiles taking over during pre-season.

Phil: Shrewsbury was the last game of another shit and disappointing season by the eleven twats and shit manager who claim to be proud of wearing the Albion colours.

They promised we'd go up automatically but we didn't even make it in the top three. The only plus-side was that we could go to the little towns and grounds and play up because the police presence was always very low profile in the lower leagues.

As any hooligan will tell you, the last game is always one of the best, if not the best. The sun is always shining and everyone meets up as they're not going to see one another for the next three months and want to play up and sign the season off on a high. About 40 to 50 of us agreed to meet at Sandwell and Dudley train station at 9.30am on the morning of the game. Everyone else would just meet us down there in Shrewsbury town centre. We met up and started our journey and while on the train an announcement was made saying they next stop was Wolverhampton. That was the signal to start playing up. Without any prompting, everyone started abusing anyone preparing to get off at the stop. About 10 more of our lads got on at that point. As the train pulled out of Wanky Wolvo, one of our lads, Britton, pulled the window down on the door and put his head out to shout more abuse. As he did it, his Burberry cap blew off down the line. "My fucking cap's gone", he said. I told him to calm down, it was only a cap but he said he'd only bought it the previous day everyone just pissed themselves laughing. I can still see the look on his face now – gutted.

We reached Shrewsbury well before 11.30am and knew the English Border Firm (EBF) wouldn't be out yet so we headed for a pub in the town centre so when they did finally get out of bed, word might just get back to them. It turned into a drinking session. We kept sending some of the younger lads out into the town centre to see if they could see Shrewsbury about yet but they were no where to be seen. By the time we marched through their town to the ground, we numbered about 130. All around the ground it was Albion everywhere. I honestly can't remember seeing any Shrewsbury colours anywhere. It was just blue and white, apart from the silly cunts in fancy dress, something I totally disagree with. If you want to wear fancy dress, have a party in your house, don't travel hundreds of miles dressed as the Pink Panther or Batman and Robin for fuck's sake.

Just as we were about to go into the ground, about 15 to 20 EBF tried to come over to me and a few lads left outside the ground. When we saw them, we started to walk over to them. One of them shouted "Come on then. Let's have it!" The little fucker knew what he was doing because the coppers heard him. "Go on", a copper said. "Do him so I can nick you, you bastard." This officer had been dying to nick me for ages but no way was I going to give him his two minutes of glory. So, feeling well pissed off, me and my mates had to walk off into the cowshed of a ground called Gay Meadow. As soon as we got in, we knew something was going to happen. The atmosphere was unreal and we knew no one gave a fuck, mainly due to the four hours of drinking I think. One, two, three, four goals Albion scored but hardly anyone was watching just talking and pissing about walking around smoking blow.

In the second half, people started climbing onto the perimeter fencing. We noticed how shit it was, and one lad, Toby, suggested we start to pull it down so about 40 to 50 lads started to pull it back and forth, even some of the shirt-wearers joined in.

The coppers came steaming over and tried pulling some of our lads onto the pitch to nick them. As soon as we ran over, the coppers would let go and we'd pull our lads back into the crowd. But this one copper had one of our lads halfway over the fence so we ran over and pulled him back by his legs. Then more coppers went over to help their colleague. So the lad was stuck on top of the fence being pulled one way by us and one way by them. I look back at that and piss myself laughing because it was like a tug of war. If it had been on You've Been Framed we'd have got £250 easily. After we pulled him back over we ran around to the side of the terraces and mingled in with the Albion fans to avoid being picked out by the police. I looked at my watch and said to Joey "When the ball comes down the wing, get everyone to jump on the pitch." Then with about two minutes to go, the ball did come down the wing and that was our cue. We all piled over what was left of the fence. The ref' and the players shit themselves and ran like fuck to the tunnel. I picked up the ball and ran into the penalty area and put it on the spot and shouted to Joey to take a penalty while I stood in goal and the next thing we knew, everyone wanted to have a go. We also decided to climb on the crossbar and when we heard it start to crack we knew it was going to snap in half. We shouted for more to come and hang off it so we could snap it. The police were more concerned at trying to stop all the shirt-wearers to kill Bobby Gould.

We couldn't get to the Shrewsbury fans because the coppers made a line about three-quarters down the pitch. Mind you, Shrewsbury didn't make an effort to have a go at us apart from about two or three of them. After about 20 minutes or so, we left the ground and found a pub just outside Shrewsbury town centre. Everyone was buzzing and the beer was flying down. But about 7.45pm a lot of people had gone back to West Brom but there were still about 12 or 13 of us left. Keron suggested we had one more in the town to see if the EBF had finally turned up so we finished our drinks off and headed into the town. We were going to go back into the pub we were in before the game when this mixed-race lad about 50ft away from us shouted "C'mon then West Brom." We knew it was a trap but being half pissed a few started to run up the hill towards him. I think the population of Shrewsbury must have been in the pub because fucking loads and loads just came running out and around the corner. The worst thing was, when we stood our ground, Shrewsbury shit themselves and started bouncing up and down and making a load of noise. So Section 5 started to walk towards them. All of a sudden, Shrewsbury started to steam down towards us. I turned around to tell everyone not to run and fucking hell, there were only about seven or eight lads left. Shrewsbury had about a 100-plus. Ado turned to me and asked what I wanted to do. I thought if we could get back to the train station we could find some sort of weapons and at least have a go back at them. So we jogged back to the train station stopping occasionally to throw a bin or a bottle that we came across in the gutter. As we got in the station, we heard a bang and saw one of their lads had tripped Ted, one of our lads, over and he'd smashed into the door. Seeing this, me, Keron and Joey ran back and jumped on him and kicked the shit out of him to make them come into the station after us. We held him by his hair and kept kicking him in the face to make them chase us up the stairs. Now they were being led into our trap.

The other lads had jumped on the train tracks and got loads of stones ready. Shrewsbury went for it and managed to get halfway up the stairs then they got pelted big time. It was brilliant as they were dropping like flies and screaming like Wolvo' girls. The best thing was that still no coppers had turned up. So after we'd fucked the EBF off I turned my attention to one of the Albion lads who had been seen hiding in a shop doorway when Ted was being battered. He got battered too and I told him never to come with us again or I'd slash his fucking face. Joey and Keron also got hold of a skinhead on a platform and made him take his laces out of his 21-hole Doc Martens and chew them until our train arrived. Watching him gag on them was quite funny really. So that was our day at Shrewsbury. I don't mind admitting they ran us because unlike the 90% of cunts who do stories, they always stood their ground and never seem to get run do they? Bullshit mate. If every firm was like they portrayed themselves in a book they'd be fighting pitched battles for hours on end with hundreds of fatalities - know what I mean?

Tony: One other firm I must mention is Burnley because in their book they said we underestimated them. KJ, one of our lads also has a bit to say about them too.

KJ: When we were relegated to the old Second Division, one of the games we looked forward to was against Burnley as we had heard they were one of the top firms in the division. We played them at Turf Moor and took a few lads. Burnley is well known for it no-nonsense police and as this game was high profile they did their best to keep us apart. After the game, there was a little scuffle as such when one of our vans full of lads got stuck in traffic but, it wasn't anything that you could say either firm got a result from. For the next game at West Brom, we knew they would turn up and they didn't disappoint. They brought two double-decker coaches but they were picked up by the Old Bill and escorted to the ground. Afterwards, they were escorted out by the police and taken to a bar called Patrick's, in Wednesbury of all places and allowed to have a drink under a heavy police presence until they were put on coaches and taken to the motorway.

Since then, some of the senior members of our firm have started travelling to England games with lads from the North West, Burnley and Rochdale areas which has led to a mutual respect and friendship between the two firms. If they play at ours, a few of their lads will meet us and stay for the weekend. A few seasons ago when we played at theirs, Eamon, Bailey and me travelled up and met Kizer, Pot and a few others and had a few drinks before and after the game. I have seen one of those Danny Dyer Football Factories programmes when they went to Burnley and met up with Pot. But he said they brought 300 lads to West Brom and "fucked us". Well, Pot, just to set the record straight. Yes, you did bring two full double-decker coaches to ours but you never fucked us because as explained earlier, we couldn't get near each other as it was well on top.

You're a good lad who always makes us feel welcome in Burnley but, hey let's keep it real. This is not me slagging Burnley off as there will always be some neutrality and mutual respect between older members of both firms.

Tony: When Burnley say we underestimated them, maybe it was because we only took a small firm in cars and did have a rough time but then again, so did all our shirt-wearing fans. We were livid. Livid we hadn't taken our proper firm and livid about all the attacks on the civilians, out of order. So for months on end afterwards all the talk was about Burnley and doing them proper when they came to ours. On the day of the game, we met at a pub pretty close to the motorway so it would be easy for them to get to us. Something they had been told about. We had a firm of about 250-300 by about 1.30/2pm, all raring to go. We then had word from them they would be arriving soon so we were all there waiting. The scene was set, so what did Burnley do? They got off the motorway in Wednesbury, four fucking miles away. Then went in a pub, made loads of noise, got beered up (Dutch courage?) and surprise, surprise attracted the Old Bill. Nice one lads - sure you didn't fancy it?

We'd told them where to come, so make your own minds up. Another thing, the lad who wrote the book says there weren't any of us about after the match. Well, the Old Bill kept you in then gave us lot the run around until we got back into West Brom where we'd had enough and turned on them leading to quite a few nickings. That's the aggro the newspapers and Old Bill referred to, not Burnley. We never saw you.

Chapter Ten

Grassing and Gassing

Tony: Mansfield away is one day I must mention. It was a hot summer's day, just before the end of the 1992/3 season. I personally thought a trip to unknown Mansfield might pull a big firm, but arriving at New Street I was surprised to see only a few. Fuck knows why. Anyway, as sometimes happens in these situations it can work out better than a big firm with not getting sussed out so quick by the OB. Well, this small but very game firm made up of me, Clem, Daz, Steve Guy, Jolly, Burf, Oaky and Turner, set off to change trains at Chesterfield. When we got there, more bad luck was to present itself. We were told that the line to Mansfield was down, so we caught a couple of cabs instead. We arranged to meet in a pub called the Swan in the market place on the High Street. Apparently Jolly had been down to a club in the town a few weeks prior and remembered the pub's name. We went in and it was pretty full considering how early it was. I was surprised at the ease at which we strolled past the doorman to go inside. As we settled down for a few jars, Steve Guy, I think it was, came back from the toilets to tell us that there was a load of lads round the corner in the pub. I think it was a sort of extension with pool tables. I also started to notice the attention the doormen were giving us and in a friendly way they told us it would probably be a good idea to leave. Reluctantly we did and thought we'd go and find another pub nearer the ground.

We walked up the side of the Swan towards a pub called the Victoria and I thought we'd definitely identified their pub as we came face-to-face with a firm of about 25-30 lads. No excuses, no lies. We bottled it I'm ashamed to say and we were on our toes. Once we had got away, and to be fair they didn't bother to chase us far, we were all gutted, shocked and very surprised with one another. None-the-less, it had happened and it was too late to put it right, or was it? We went to another pub by the ground before kick-off but we really couldn't get to grips with what had happened, after all we were all game lads. We won the game 3-0 and various people had been told what had happened earlier. But, only one thing was going to change the outcome of that and it came in the shape of another one of our top boys, Eamon Payne, the younger brother of John, who has already been mentioned in the book for his top fighting skills and reputation. Eamon was pretty notorious himself by now, with England as well as Albion, and a gamer lad you could not find. When he heard what had gone on he too couldn't believe we'd run. It was obvious to him that we would have to go back to the Swan.

We had a few drinks in a quiet back-street pub towards Mansfield town centre and I remember thinking this was a suicide mission. We'd seen at least 50 of their boys earlier, on top of the 20-odd by the Swan, now there were the original eight of us plus Eamon. I even tried to put it to Eam' that it wasn't a good idea but he wouldn't have it so if he was going so would we, fuck it. Eventually the football crowds and traffic disappeared and we were bowlin' down the road towards the Swan. This time, no matter how many were in there I knew we wouldn't budge. It was strangely silent and empty in the street by the pub but when I saw the boozer the old stomach was churning. I knew this was going to be a mad one. There were no doormen and inside we discovered there was no fucker in there except a few in-breds and the odd couple.

We were totally gob-smacked and talk about a let down, or relief. We got our drinks and sat down by the entrance. A local kid came over and started chatting. He wasn't a lad so we humoured him. About 10 minutes or so passed and I still kept getting the feeling something was going to happen. I said so to Stevie Guy and no sooner as I did we looked and there through the glass, double doors were dozens of heads popping up around the windows and doors. Obviously we had been sussed and I reckoned on this was it.

Only two lads walked in and strangely enough headed straight to Eamon who was sitting down looking very calm. Then a bloke, a boxer-type asked him "Are we going to have a drink or are we having fun today?" It was like a red rag to a bull. Eam' practically knocked him into the next postcode. He went out through the doors, as did the locals, and we all followed with stools and glasses. As we ran after them we caught a few of the braver ones and kicked the fuck out of them. But they'd gone. Just like that. As we walked back towards the pub, pumped up to fuck, a big roar went up behind us - their re-enforcements had arrived. Eamon shouted to stand, which every last one did, Daz Guy and Clem being particularly good in these situations. We were now well up for it, fists and boots flying in all directions but still we gave as good as we got, if not better. Apart from Turner getting knocked out, they seemed to be carrying all the injuries and the fighting stopped with them backing away, even clapping us and asking us to come for a drink with them. We declined, we ain't soft. Anyway we'd got our revenge and had put what happened earlier to bed and no doubts about who saved the day. Fair-play to each and every one of us. It took a lot of guts to do what we did, but it really was down to one man's stubbornness - Eamon Payne. Stubbornness I've witnessed time and time again battling side-by-side with the lad. Unbelievable bottle.

As you'd expect, the police soon arrived and said that although we'd done so well we had to leave Mansfield, now. So they kindly got us taxis to Chesterfield and that was that as they say, or was it? When we arrived at the station we made our way to the Birmingham-bound platform. We were talking about what had gone on and were feeling pretty pleased with ourselves. The train pulled in after about 10 minutes or so and about eight or 10 lads got off. They looked slightly like football lads, a bit tramp-ish looking though. One of them looked at me as our paths crossed and asked me what I was looking at. Bang! Clem was already switched on. The lad never stood a chance as he put him on his arse with a sweet right. That was it, with the mouth piece put away they just ran for it in any direction before they came back and we chased them again and so on, lasting for about five minutes. They were really wank.

But as luck would have it, due to the train being held up the Old Bill arrived with the Chesterfield lads in tow clutching various parts of their injured bodies and pointing us out. I couldn't catch my breath. I always assumed the unwritten law of never grassin' on other football lads had reached as far as Derbyshire. They nicked four of us and after we were charged and appeared in court for affray/breach of the peace and assault, we were obviously made aware of their statements. You wouldn't believe what these pathetic excuses for a football firm had said about what had gone on. We had apparently attacked them, unprovoked, beat up a girl who was with them and there were about 30 of us and they feared for their lives. Fucking 30 - in two taxis?

On the day of the trial, their main boy, Joey Revel I think his name was, stood there and swore our lives away with a right load of shite. What a wanker. They actually wanted us banged up for it. Shame on your boys Chesterfield. However, there were too many lies and we all got found not guilty. So, in our eyes the infamous Chesterfield Bastard Squad became the Chesterfield Grassin' Squad. We did actually tell some of their lads about what happened a few months later when we were on our way to Rotherham. About 100 of us got off in Chesterfield and we knew they were at home, so we went to a pub called the Crooked Spire by the famous landmark of the same name. The Old Bill soon parked up nearby and kept an eye on us. A few of their spotters came to talk to us and we told them what had gone on. Surprisingly they said they knew nothing of it. A few of them kept driving past in cars and having a nose but they knew they couldn't fuck with us so we fucked off to our train after an hour and that's the last time we ever met up with them. Luckily for them. I wonder if they ever said anything to Revel? Probably not, probably all the same.

* * * * * * *

Early '94 saw Stoke City come to the Hawthorns. Historically, there is usually always trouble at this fixture and Albion have always turned out for it and this day was to be no exception. A few of us were drinking around West Brom and as usual we ended up in the Lewisham pub at the very top of the High Street. Some of the older lads, the old Smethwick mob, had told us about 50-60 Stoke had tried to get in there early doors but the Old Bill had diffused the situation and escorted them towards the ground. At around 2.15pm, a large mob of us set off towards the ground and, as anyone will tell you it's quite a hike and takes up to 20 minutes. I noticed a bus arrive as we were walking towards the motorway island and I saw Eamon, Clem, Peachy and a few others jump on it. I didn't give it much thought at the time and just carried on chin-wagging about things all football lads discuss "Think we'll find 'em?" and "Think it'll go off?"

As time moved on, I must admit I'd lost hope of anything happening. My guess was the Old Bill had put them in the ground. As we approached the ground, we got caught up in the crowds queuing to get in. You see, at the time our firm all used to sit in the stand past the Brummie Road called the Rainbow - what a poxy name - so we had to get through the congestion. As we reached the end of the Brummie, I can still remember saying "Where the fuck are they?" to a lad called Crogey. But, before I blinked he punched a lad in front of me. Fucking hell, they were stood smack-bang in front of us, giving it loads. I lashed out catching one in the mouth. His mate then repaid the compliment, opening my bottom lip up. It was bang-off proper now, total chaos all around, a toe-to-toe free-for-all. I then clocked Eamon and others steam in from the side, having just got off the bus. Fists were flying everywhere as we drove 'em back all the way round to the Rainbow. The police were trying desperately to intervene but both firms were going hell for leather. The ferocity of our attack seemed to be taking its toll as Stoke's firm looked a beaten one. The police on horseback waded in to break up what had become a very noisy, bloody battle. People started to run to avoid them as they put a line between us with the horses. I thought everyone else had the same idea as me and like a prat I dived through a gap between the horses, pretty much leaving me on my own. Punches and kicks rained down on me from all angles from Stoke. I tried to get free but it was soon over as I was dived on by officers from the Operational Support Unit – the old Special Patrol Group - and dragged through a turnstile. I tried in vain to get away but they gave me a torrid time, you always try to plead your innocence but to no avail. I was later charged with a very laughable Section 18 wounding with intent and breach of the peace. The copper apparently broke his finger punching me on the back of the head so I felt he tried to stitch me up. I kept going not guilty, and they did drop the wounding to ABH and then found me guilty of that and breach of the peace. Sentencing was adjourned for a couple of months for reports and I was told to expect another custodial sentence but, not before another relegation battle which saw us having to beat Portsmouth at Fratton Park, on the last day of the season.

As always on these days the kick-off was on a Sunday which isn't all bad as it gives you all plenty of time to get down there by going down on the Saturday. Everyone knows Pompey are a serious firm but it seems not everyone rates little old West Brom. Suits us though as we have loved putting the so-called "rated" firms in their places over the years. So, it was on the Saturday a decent size firm of about 25 met in West Brom and travelled down in cars to Southsea and after finding digs, did what all good football lads do and went on the pop.

I wasn't amongst this lot but have been told it wasn't long into the night before they bumped into some of the Pompey's lads outside a pub. The Pompey boys fronted them and our lot were only too glad to accommodate them. Bottles, chairs, fists, glasses and CS gas was used in the first meaningful skirmish of the night. Needless to say, it soon attracted the attention of the police who sent our boys on their way.

Portsmouth knew Albion were in Southsea and it wasn't long before they found each other again, this time outside a nightclub. Again both sides, with roughly equal numbers of about 50, were equally as game. This time however the fighting lasted sometime, spilling out further along the front as both firms fought to get the upper hand. Our boys kept unloading more and more gas at Pompey which understandably seemed to give them the upper hand. Eventually the Old Bill arrived and again and dispersed the two firms this time arresting a few lads and also insisting that Albion lads went back to their B&Bs or face a night in the cells. Tough choice ay? They settled for the digs. Some of the lads were in their rooms skinning up and having a few beers later on when they heard shouting outside. It was Pompey throwing bricks and shouting for our lot to come out and fight. Trouble was, as our lot charged out to join them the police again intervened so it was goodnight, see you all in the morning.

On the morning of the game, a coach load of lads from the Whiteheath and Blackheath areas and me and a few others arrived safely in Southsea. It didn't take us long to find our comrades and to find out what had gone the previous night. A few carried fresh wounds which reminded me of just where we were. We found a bar on the seafront with a few tables and chairs outside and soon loads of whiz and charlie were flying about. As the morning went by, more and more lads joined up with us, taking our numbers to around the 100 mark. As the time approached for us to leave for Fratton Park, I couldn't believe we hadn't come across any Portsmouth lads especially as they knew exactly where we were. We didn't see any en route either. We got to the ground about 15 minutes before kick-off only to find the away end overflowing and locked. But to our amazement, the Old Bill told us to follow them towards the home end. We were led in and discovered they had pushed the home fans back to almost the halfway line, rolled some police tape from the top to the bottom of the terrace, put a few stewards and the odd bobby in and that was it. So you'd got West Brom's main firm and Pompey's separated by fucking tape. How long was that going to last? About five minutes is all, and we were through giving Pompey a right pasting. Don't get me wrong, they were just as game. As this seething, violent mass of bodies clashed it spilled onto the pitch and held up kick-off. Police came from all angles to try and quell the fighting. Some fans ran from all parts of the ground to join in and it seemed to take ages to stop as the Old Bill had to push Pompey fans even further back due to the Albion lads gaining more of the terrace. Again and again during the game Albion steamed through the police only to be beaten back. The one thing I couldn't get my head around was the fact nobody was getting arrested - although plenty were getting led away by St. John's Ambulance.

At the end of the game, which we won 1-0 and therefore stayed up, celebrating Albion lads clashed with their local counterparts on the pitch, albeit briefly. Eventually we were all pushed back to the terrace and we stayed behind for a while to wait for the crowds to filter away. About 80 of us had to head to Southsea and as we made our way through the terraced streets we picked up a few more lads who'd made their way down in cars or train. There were plenty of Albion fans celebrating everywhere and someone came back to tell us a firm of Pompey were up ahead. We approached a green with shops all around it and there they were and loads of Old Bill who, on seeing us, drove the Pompey fans back towards Southsea whilst keeping us at bay. But after about 10 minutes they finally realised they had to let us go the same way but separately. As we walked down the winding streets toward Southsea, I noticed a small mob of about 20 Pompey lads following us about 100-150 yards behind us. I told some of our lads and about 20 of us hid up a side street behind some parked cars, whilst the rest of our firm planned to spread across the road around the bend. Obviously they couldn't see around the bend so wouldn't see the ambush coming. As they walked around the winding street they came face-to-face with a dwindled firm of Albion spread across their path. They stopped dead in their tracks as about 20 of us steamed into them from the rear. One of ours, DG, caught the first lad across the head with a coping stone he'd ripped off a garden wall. We tore into them from both sides and credit due to them they tried to put up a good resistance, except for one lad who ducked and dived his way out and away. They took a ferocious beating with one of our black contingent, ML, giving one of them an almighty penalty kick to the head before shouting "Smethwick!" Well, he enjoyed it.

As was always going to happen, police came from all ways with dogs, the lot and rounded us up whilst treating the injured in the aftermath. Obviously peeved at us, they escorted us all back to Southsea where the welcoming party of the 657 Crew were getting the run-around from the Old Bill. It was a pretty hairy few minutes trying to get to the cars and diving in any car nearby. Ours was overflowing with Mart driving, me, Easty, Wilf, then our hitchhikers from Smethwick, Marshall, Ruddy and Garfield - none of us small lads by any stretch of the imagination. We drove the latter back to Fratton train station where somebody decided to relieve a Pompey lad of a nice Aquascutum coat. Overall it was job done, staying up and giving Pompey a proper surprise. Over the years Pompey have been a top firm but, like so many others, underestimated West Brom at their peril. Their local rag described it as the worst ever crowd violence inside Fratton Park.

In the October of that year I was up for sentencing for ABH on a copper and breach of the peace from Stoke, as mentioned earlier. I was given a six-month prison sentence and another 12-month football banning order, my fourth one. As my heart sank and I winked at my pal trying to look not bothered, a probation officer suddenly jumped to his feet and asked permission to address the court. He was allowed and began to tell the magistrates of this new course they were running called Anger Management. They had apparently introduced it to help people like myself overcome things such as football violence. The bench listened, then kept looking over at me and finally decided to give me an amazing choice. If I agreed to go on a probation order, attend the course and pay a heavy fine they would scrap the jail sentence. After careful deliberation (not) I went for the jail. As if, I snatched their hands off mate, who wouldn't? I was so relieved to be heading out the door of the West Brom courts and not into Winson Green that day, I can tell you. It worked out very well for me to be honest. I was probably more gutted about the ban at the time.

I stuck to all conditions except one, the anger management course, because someone attending it attacked the bloke who ran it. Must've worked then. It was around this time that I met and fell for my future wife, Vanessa. She was very aware of me and my pals' activities up the Albion and not exactly happy with it. The ban kicked in on 20 October 1994 so that was it for 12 months. To be fair, during the following year I wasn't active up the Albion. I moved out of West Brom and in with Vanessa in Stourbridge where life became a lot easier for me. We bought a flat together and all was going great but as the 12 months ended it was back up the football. The first game was Leicester City at home. It was funny to see suddenly that all and sundry had a mobile phone to their ear arranging battles. I had to lay low for a while, which is what I did especially as the football intelligence officer welcomed me back with a warning that they would be taking a special interest in my movements. He is a big, fat Scotsman by the name of Frank Carling. He was okay with me at times but could be a bit of a bastard to some of the others. I would say he was "looking after us" for about 10 years until he handed over the reigns to Keith Parks. I suppose these two would have some good stories to tell about us lot but I've refrained from asking them.

West Bromwich is only a small town compared with others that house football clubs but it has a decent sized firm. The trouble is a big police force is also present in West Brom and they have been all over us for years, with all our top boys having constant hassle from Carling, Parksy and Co. I couldn't name one of our firm who hasn't been banned, not one. All firms encounter hassle from the law and constant observation - our police might as well be living with us, fucking nightmare. But none-the-less, we kept at it springing surprise after surprise. Even today there is an active firm of young lads - known as "The Youth" - getting the same shite as we did but off a new officer called Portman. Good luck to them all, they'll need it.

PART FIVE

Chapter Eleven

New Faces

*B*ig Jon has been following the Albion since he was a young lad and
although on the fringes of the firm from the mid-Eighties, didn't get
fully involved for another decade. However, he played a large part in
organising and liaising with the sometimes divided groups that existed within
the West Brom mob, which wasn't without its problems as he explains.

Jon: I was born in Birmingham in December 1967. My father was from
the Handsworth Wood area of Birmingham and my mother from
Ward End. I have two sisters and I am the only lad although I do also
have step-brothers. I grew up in the King Norton area of Birmingham
in what was a turbulent household because basically my father was
violent towards my mother and anyone else that cared to cross his
path. He was basically a bully. After he left, our household life was
bliss, our life became normal and our mother was our heroine, she did
a grand job of bringing us up and we never went without anything.
Years on, she now lives abroad with a very comfortable lifestyle with a
very good man so all's well that ends well. I visit her on a regular basis
and she is a very big part of my life.

I went to school in the local area and eventually left school with
five O' Levels. During my youth, I attended many West Brom games
with my father. He relayed stories of trouble at games in his younger
days so my introduction to football violence was verbal. At quite an
early age, I became fairly streetwise and understood what was going
on around me in my local area and at football games. In 1983 I went
to the West Brom v Millwall League Cup game at the Hawthorns. I

was 15 and that night opened my eyes to serious crowd disorder. The thing was, it did not frighten me it gave me a buzz and watching West Brom and Millwall thugs knocking lumps out of each other was more entertaining than the game - which we won 5-1. After the game, my father and I had to walk through the Millwall hordes in Halfords Lane. It was a sight to be seen. They were throwing anything they could get their hands on at the Old Bill and any other people they saw. Walking through this lot was a scary experience I admit. I could not get my breath at how lawless they were and were intent on serious violence. When we were some distance away, I looked back up the road to witness the sight of the Old Bill in the middle and West Brom lads on the other side launching missiles at the Millwall lot. This made me proud and was the very beginnings of my extreme loyalty towards the club I love.

I left school at 16 and went straight into work on a building site. It was tough work but the money was good and I was also in the process of joining the Army. Eventually after being messed about by the recruitment people my application fell through due to a medical problem with my eyes. I was gutted because being a soldier had always been an ambition of mine. I got over my disappointment and got on with my job on the building site. Obviously at this stage I was a young man with plenty of money so I got into going to games every week, both at home and away, with numerous lads from my area. We had a great time travelling country-wide without a care in the world. We travelled on the supporter's coaches for the first few years and there was a good crowd of us and to be honest, trouble in these initial couple of years was fairly rare. It was just minor skirmishes, although we did have scary experiences at certain places like West Ham and Spurs because anything to them was a target. When I was 19, I left the building game. It was too much hard work especially in the winter when work was not always guaranteed and I joined a large distribution company where I remain to this day. This job has stood me in good stead for all of the years I have worked there and financially it has helped set me up for life. My earnings were now even better and I drifted away from travelling on the coaches and started travelling on the train or in cars again with lads from my local area and some from work, usually about 10 of us went.

It was clear at a fair few games that rivalries existed amongst the lads that formed Albion's firm. There always seemed to be bad vibes for some reason and we often witnessed fights between our own lads.

This was not very welcoming at all and numerous times we were the victims of our own people with very bad attitudes. Because of the bad vibes, we decided that we would stick together and not get involved in the inner-circle, if you like. We drank away from them at home games and never ventured into West Bromwich. We drank in Handsworth or in pubs next to the ground. Eventually these bad attitudes took their toll and several of my pals fell by the wayside and drifted away from the firm and the scene. I could not blame them but I was a stubborn so-and-so and I stuck with it with some pals but we still never joined in with the main lot. I knew quite a few faces and always exchanged nods but because of the way it was I could not be arsed to make a lot of effort in building bridges. We just carried on doing our own thing.

Over the years, I have witnessed this with many small groups of Albion lads.

Suspicion is always in evidence when strange faces are present within the firm. They are not welcome to this day and this, in my opinion, has prevented Albion being the firm it should be. I think the main problem is you have so many lads from so many different areas - all of the districts in West Bromwich as well as all the surrounding areas like Dudley, Stourbridge, Kidderminster, Blackheath, Bearwood, Smethwick and many, many more. There are also plenty lads from Birmingham which again causes some friction because of Brummie/ Black Country rivalries and general dislike of each other.

As we got into the Nineties, I was still attending many games but I, along with pals from my area, had got into the loved-up era. My pals made big money when they were involved in this. I went along for the good times and women and with work and other sidelines, I was making very good money on my own and did not need finance from the proceeds of drugs and promoting raves and door security. I did do door-work off and on but, that was more of a favour for a pal who had his own door firm. I have never considered myself to be a hard-man or an old type doorman who cracked heads for fun. I was employed more as a bit of a thinker with the ability to defuse situations verbally. I could handle myself if needed but I was no superman and the clubs where we worked attracted some very moody characters. The plus-points were always the fact that most of my pals were very well respected throughout the Midlands and further a field so trouble – on a big scale - was very rare. I continued to go to games and we continued to latch onto the firm for big games. Some of these games are covered by the other lads in the book.

Around 1992/3, I became friendlier with a big Albion character from my local area. Alfie was well known amongst Albion's firm and he had been part of the Clubhouse. He knew everyone involved up the Albion and he was well liked. I started going to games with him, mainly due to the fact my mates had now had enough of all the bollocks and knocked it all on the head. We became big friends very quickly and I became part of his circle. Most of this group were from Bearwood and included the Caswell brothers, Alan and Ant, Jonah, Kev Dent, Kenny (my future brother-in-law), Mark Thompson (Fowks) Steve, brothers John and Jim amongst others. These were sound lads and very loyal to one another. We started travelling everywhere together by car and on trains for the big games when the whole firm was present. Being around these lads opened the door for me to get in with all the lads. This Bearwood group were well known and well liked within the inner-circles of the firm. I had finally cracked it after close on 10 years of trying to get my face in and known. I got to know more and more lads as time went on. I didn't get involved in any verbal planning or any of that really, I just kept my mouth shut and got on with things. After a while we started travelling more and more with other lads from Oldbury, the likes of brothers Steve and Daz Guy and other lads from Blackheath, such as Big Dave and the Shaw Brothers. Another lad, Mickey R, who was from area also knocked about with these lads. They were all sound and very reliable in all situations. I regard Daz as one of Albion's main faces from all the time I spent up there, no-nonsense, straight to the point geezer and very handy with it. All of them are massive Albion fans first and foremost and that gets my respect from the very beginning.

In my opinion, football hooligans fall into several categories. This is no cover up or excuse for the violence that occurs excuses are pointless. Firstly, you have your nutcase who has a little local pride and tags onto the team or firm to fulfil his violent needs. Then you have your earners who tag along with bigger firms on the rob, usually clothes shops or pub tills and the like. Then you have my category, my soul intention is to follow West Bromwich Albion football club, my interest is in the team doing the best it can all of the time. I have spent many thousands of pounds following my team. If violence was my intention I could easily save money and sit in my local waiting for a fight to start. My outlook has always been the same. If someone wants to fight me because I am Albion then I will oblige big time with maximum force and maximum violence. If that is not the case, then

I am always happy to watch the game, socialise afterwards and go home pissed and happy.

In 1995 I met a local Bearwood girl, things developed rather quickly and in 1996 we moved in together to a flat in Bearwood. I was fairly happy but never really settled and I seriously had my doubts but things were okay and 1997 we were married. In 1998 we bought a house in Oldbury and things were good but I still had my doubts and even though living in this area meant I was even further in with the firm and I knew more faces, I was homesick for my local area. Shortly afterwards my wife lost a baby and after this, our relationship went rapidly down hill. I must be brutally honest here. Football was one of my main interests and leading up to games from the mid-Nineties my phones were red-hot with planning, this was obviously not much fun for her but to be frank I didn't care less. I worked all week and Saturday was football. She came a very bad second. In 2001 the relationship had completely fallen apart. To be honest, me seeing a girl from work and another through the football did not help matters but the marriage was long over before they developed into naughtiness. Later that year, I finally had enough and collected anything worth taking from the house and left on my way back to Kings Norton. I was chuffed to be out of it really, life is too short to be bitter but I consider I wasted five to six years for nothing. To this day I blame myself because I should have listened to my own doubts and fears. Lesson learned and no going back.

In the months that followed this I was in trouble on three counts. Firstly, for driving offences that threatened my livelihood, secondly, I was in court for assault charges after a bust-up with my ex and someone else and thirdly, I was in trouble on a charge of self-defence with excessive force after an incident on the door of a bar/club in Newquay A very good brief got me a good result on the driving offences - six points and a big fine and a huge sigh of relief. They got the assault charges thrown out of court after a comical show by the prosecution witnesses that still makes me chuckle to this day. The other charges never came to court after the Old Bill viewed the CCTV footage and noted the ferocious attack on us. However, we were warned never to work there again. Going back to the Nineties and football, I was well in with the firm. West Brom don't travel as a firm on a regular basis, only for big games. Divisions I witnessed in my early years still exist today and I have a feeling they will always remain, sad but true. I was on friendly terms with a whole host of lads from the games. My friends from Bearwood will always remain my loyal and best friends

- Alfie in particular but I was also good friends with a whole host of other lads. Whilst living in Oldbury, I became good friends with all the Albion lads from that area, people like Phil E, Steve G, Carl C, Dougy B, Connor, Lynx, Keith and others. Most of these lads were up there with some of the best lads we have. They were always there when violence was on the agenda and several of us used to get our heads together and organise things.

I'd say that our firm, at home for big games, was always well organised and we had good quality faces out and at times for particular games our numbers were enormous. We always stuck together and I am fully aware that this particular group taking on the mantle of organising things did put a fair few peoples' noses out of joint. Several rumours surfaced from time to time to try to discredit us. The rumours came at a bad time for me. I was going through a messy divorce and it was around the time of the three charges so being accused of being a grass is not nice especially when the people spreading those rumours did not have the balls to say it to my face. Cowards of the highest order who, in my opinion, were simply jealous of our close-knit firm organising things and wanted us to break up and implode. These grassing jibes were categorically unfounded nonsense. I have never done anybody wrong up the games, neither would I. I admit that during 2001-2002 my behaviour was a little strange. I'd start to organise coaches etc then simply lose interest and knock it on the head and during our first Premiership season we were very active at home for the first few months of the season. I hung back away from the front line of fights because I was on bail for one charge and had another hanging over me. One more arrest would undoubtedly mean being remanded in jail and to be quite honest, I did not fancy that.

This did not go unnoticed by some and the rumour mill swung fully into action. At first, I was massively insulted by this, bearing in mind my experiences in my early years of going to games with my pals and having trouble with our supposed own should have stood me in good stead. It did not and from 2003 onwards I knocked it on the head completely going back to my teenage ways of doing things - going to games with local pals and sticking with them. But when these accusations surfaced, loads of our lads approached me and gave me their support. I appreciated that greatly and it will never be forgotten.

From 2003 onwards, my interest in the firm was zero. I still had contact with all of my pals but getting involved in any trouble or organising was the furthest thing from my mind. I did get talked into a few scrapes with Cardiff, home and away, and obviously the Uplands incident with Villa, which there is more on in later chapters.

We paid dearly for that day. I had a choice there though. I could easily have driven away and left the lads to it but I looked down the road and saw lads like Phil, Carl, Chinda, Keith, Bail, Connor, Eamon and Clem and I simply could not do it. My loyalty to these people was still there. I was the first one to see the camera but I could not leave. Some did but I could not.

I still have an extreme loyalty to West Bromwich Albion. My first game was at the age of three and I have been to well over a thousand games now and visited 86 grounds since and I have also followed England all over the world. Included in my entries for this book are some of the good days and a few bad ones. Unlike a lot of these books, I will be perfectly honest. I've been done plenty times following Albion and England and I also had one hell of a beating from South Yorkshire's riot police which is covered in one of my passages. Shit happens but I can be honest and say that on our day with all of our faces present, we are a match for most, not all but most. Simple as that.

In January 2004, I plucked up the courage to ask a girl from work out and we have been together for nearly four years now and she is my absolute rock. Whilst in prison she was a tower of strength she looked after everything and was there for me 100%. I will be forever grateful for all she has done for me - she has restored my faith in women. In October 2005, her father passed away whilst I was in jail. This was a huge kick in the bollocks for me. He was Karen's dad and her best friend. I felt useless because I could not be there for her and I will always regret that. The future is marriage for us and when my ban is lifted I will be taking our children to games. My time is finished. At times it was great - the friendships and loyalties will always remain and I will remember those good times rather than the bad. RIP Colin R Kemp. I will look after your little girl today and always...

Chapter Twelve
Punch-ups and Play-offs

Jon: In May 1999, we travelled up to Tranmere in a 17-seater minibus. Amongst the 17 were, Tony Freeth, Daz G, Micky R, Big Alfie, Kendo, Adam C, Paul U, Jamie, Big Dave, Leggy, Sharky and Danksy. There had been a bit of history with Tranmere with them having a go at the Clipper pub right outside their ground mainly after the game when most away fans would have left and gone home. Amusingly enough, Tranmere had come unstuck on a few occasions during these incidents mainly against our shirts. I don't know where the bad feeling came from. It could have started when they travelled to ours years previously and had a bad time in Smethwick. I recall someone was stabbed and they were chased up the train tracks. Anyway, back to the day in question. I cannot remember anything about the journey up there and I was sober as a judge because I was driving the van. We arrived near the ground and parked up about a five minute walk away from the ground behind a boozer called the Sportsman, where we would later have some fun and games. Our walk to the ground was trouble-free and after watching the game we went into the Clipper pub as mentioned above. There were a fair few Albion lads about and loads of shirts. We drank outside the pub and noticed we were being clocked by locals and then some of Tranmere's lads approached us. We were up and ready for action but due to Old Bill close by it was no more than a show of strength and a bit of verbal from both sides.

They left the area rather sharp-ish when they saw our numbers and intention to give them a slap. It ended with them instructing us to let things go quiet and then to come to the pub up the road. Yep, you've guessed it, where we'd parked the van.

After about an hour things had died down. Most Albion had drifted away leaving us 17 from the van and a few other lads who were on the train. We totalled just over 20 no more than 25. We left the Clipper and walked up the hill towards the pub and our van. My feelings were that if it did go off and the Old Bill were involved, we had the perfect excuse that our van was parked there and we were on our way back to it when all hell broke loose - an excuse which worked later. We approached the pub and were about 100 yards away when they clocked us. The shout of "They're here" must have gone up in the pub because about 40 to 50 of them came piling out and spread out across the road. We adopted the usual Albion tactic over the years, no shouting or running just calmly walking towards them. We came to within 30-40 yards of them and had also spread out across the road. We took a casualty early on in the proceedings when Paul U took a full bottle of Lucozade in the face. It knocked him clean out and he was face down on the pavement. This gave them a gee-up and some confidence and fuck me, the lot came at us, bricks, bottles, glasses. Bearing in mind the numbers difference I found this rather strange because they outnumbered us at least two or three to one and I wondered why they had not simply just come into us.

The row continued with us returning everything they had thrown at us and slaps being handed out mainly by our lot but not on a major scale. To be perfectly honest, it was mainly a throwing match but due to our numbers we had to hold firm otherwise we could have come badly unstuck. They were just bouncing around throwing things but they still wouldn't come into us. We pushed them back to virtually outside the pub. I'd managed to get a few digs in as had Daz G and a few others. They were starting to flap a little because we were not budging and we were the ones throwing the punches and all their missile throwing had not made any difference. We need to bear in mind here we were one lad down and we were fighting and trying to help him up at the same time and, to be perfectly truthful some of our lot - from the train - had also flapped it and not got involved. This was bad news and I let them know that before it had gone off. Their excuse was the numbers difference, a poor show in my eyes. I won't mention names but they know who they are. After roughly three or four minutes of the row going off, the OB started to arrive. It was just two officers at first and they couldn't stop it so they simply observed and radioed for help. We pushed Tranmere back even further and started to give out more slaps. They were coming under increasing pressure so we then took our chance and all charged forward. They simply scattered in all directions. We didn't give chase as it was a case of job done. In a nutshell, we were a man down early doors and 15-16 of us had held off at least double our numbers and done a decent job.

Anyone who has travelled to football games through all the divisions will know that firms such as Tranmere exist in loads of towns and cities across the country. This was no major victory. We stood firm, confident that the 17 in that van would not let each other down. The Old Bill nicked two of ours and Paul U had to go to hospital with a bit of a gash and a sore head. Our day in the Wirral ended with us picking up Paul U from the hospital after he discharged himself and then Daz G and Kendo from the police station when they were released with a caution. The excuse I mentioned earlier about us returning to the van had worked. We said we were attacked but the Old Bill said it looked like Tranmere were being attacked not us. He was right but, shit happens. A good day and for the record, amongst those 17 lads in that van were two or three of Albion's best lads and the rest are all sound. Stand-on lads and apologies to anyone I have missed out, no disrespect intended. We stopped off in Stafford on the way home and had a laugh about the day's events and sank a few beers.

* * * * * * *

For England v Scotland play-off at Glasgow in November, me and Phil E organised a coach. We met at the Rising Sun pub in West Bromwich town centre the night before the game and we departed at drinking up time and headed north with one of the best Albion firms - faces-wise - I ever had the pleasure of being part of. We had lads from Great Barr, Cradley Heath, Blackheath, Bearwood, Quinton, Rowley Regis, Nuneaton, Stourbridge, Tipton as well as others in West Bromwich. We also had a couple of Villa lads present who were pals of some of our lads from Cradley. They are hated rivals of ours but England is a different kettle of fish. It doesn't always happen but everyone should be as one for England games especially in games such as this. I had previously travelled to Glasgow in '85, '87 and '89 and these games were pretty eventful to say the least in fact, the '87 game is to this day still the most violence I have ever witnessed and been involved in. England completely swamped the place in '87 and severely took the piss. So, for this one we headed north with the beer and white stuff in full flow. It was an uneventful journey and we arrived in Glasgow at 5am on the day of the game. We were dropped off in the city centre and arranged for the driver to pick us up in Hamilton that evening. We headed up towards the market areas known as the Barrowlands because with it being the market area the pubs and bars are open early if indeed they ever shut. We were halfway up towards the Barrowlands when in the distance we spotted a decent sized firm stood at the road side. When we got up close to them it became apparent it was Birmingham City's lads, the Zulus, numbering 60-70. There is no real bad blood between us. We have had numerous incidents with them over the years but a lot of lads on both sides know each other and there is a mutual respect. Personally, I know a fair few of their lads and some of them were with this firm. We walked past without incident and a few conversations were had between each other. I could go into detail about one of our former lads who had defected to Blues and was with this firm. He did his best to hide amongst them but he was noticed. He doesn't deserve a write up and is no serious loss at all. My only point is, you do not shit on your own doorstep. He has, numerous times and that will catch up with him one day.

We got ourselves into a café and all filled up ready to carry on with the beer and the long day ahead. I was then approached by some of the Blues faces from earlier wanting to know what our intentions were for the day. I said I couldn't speak for everyone but our feelings were that we were all there as England and that was it but, if we bumped into Wolves or Villa obviously local issues could come to a head and it was very likely it would go off. They were amused by this, wished us well and carried on back to the rest of their lot. After leaving the café we had a look about for a bar/pub that was open and it wasn't long before we found one and we all went in. We were the only people in there apart from a few locals and bearing in mind the vast majority of our lads had been drinking from the previous evening you can imagine the mood. It was play-up mode and with the barmy Spencer present it was bound to be an eventful session. After a while, I noticed a couple of figurines of Gerry Adams and Martin McGuinness behind the bar. This didn't go down too well at all and the mood turned a little nasty from this point on. Obviously the Barrowlands is in close proximity to Celtic park and is basically a staunch Fenian area. I've seen this area smashed to bits by England and I think this bar was very quickly coming onto our hit list. I went outside for some air and there was a handful of our lot out there and I joined them for a chat and a laugh. It wasn't long before we noticed a group of quite well dressed lads on the opposite side of the road numbering 10-15 and we tried to suss out who they were. The Old Bill had been milling about in uniform so we didn't want to confront them at this early stage. We waited a little to see what would happen and at this point one of our main faces Johnny P came out of the pub to join us. He saw the group too but without hesitation steamed straight over the road and confronted them with us lot not too far behind him. You have probably guessed it, but they were plain clothes OB. It was fucking hilarious. He was a man possessed. He, along with his brother Eamon, is up there with the gamest lads I have ever seen at football games. They are both sound and Johnny can seriously battle and Eamon is not too far behind. The OB pulled Johnny, cautioned and searched him and luckily let him go. He was very lucky because not only had he confronted them but they had failed to find something he had stashed in his bag.

The mood in the pub continued in the same vein. The more the beer flowed, the songs started - anti-IRA and Loyalist-England songs were repeated. The manager and bar staff were not at all impressed but the money was being spent so they put up with it. Our numbers grew steadily throughout the morning. We were joined by more of our lads who had travelled up by car and train. By 11am we numbered close on 70. We had also been joined by some pals of Eamon from Burnley, Kaizer and a few others. I'd met them before and they were good lads. At about midday we decided to move closer down towards the city centre. Before we left the pub fire hoses were set off and pushed into the electrics which blew the lot. The gaffer and staff were even more pissed off now but shit happens and I think bearing in mind those figurines, if the OB had not been about on a regular basis the place would have been smashed to bits.

We walked back through the market area back down towards the outskirts of the city centre and plotted up in another bar. Some Palace lads were in there and we had a chat with them and carried on with the beer consumption. We stayed until 1.30pm and then all headed off further into the city centre. Along the way we encountered a firm of Reading who included the idiot off the Chelsea TV documentary. They were a bit lippy but were mostly youngsters so we left alone and carried on our way. After this day, on the grapevine these Reading fools were said to refer to our lot as a "Paki" firm. We had a couple of Indian lads with us as West Brom is a multi-racial firm and there are no issues of race or colour between each other. Colour does not come into question, at the end of the day we are all on the same side. These "Paki" jibes were to come back and bite these Reading fools on the arse a few years later when we played them at theirs for the last game of the season. We took an enormous firm, hundreds, but the OB swarmed all over us. Ten of our lot including Chinda and Khulla (the Indian lads) entered Reading's pub and took 20 of them apart but that's another story.

Anyway, we were now on our way into the city centre we turned the corner into a side street. I was more or less at the back of our lot and as I came around the corner this little side street was basically in chaos. Our lot were fighting, with who I do not know and as we all pushed forward the opposition turned and ran. Some ran away from us and roughly half of them ran into a pub half way up the side street slamming some iron gates behind them. We immediately attacked the pub, we couldn't get inside due to the gates but we tried to rip them off. The Jocks were inside the gates throwing glasses, bottles and anything else they could get their hands on. I took a bottle full in the face. It shattered on the gates and sprayed my face with little shards of glass. The next thing I knew, the Old Bill were swarming all over us. They gathered us all together and lined us up against the wall. I thought we were nicked. They searched us all, held us for a short time and then let us all go. I could not believe it. We later learnt the firm that we faced in the side street were Hibbs. This was a bit of a coup because Hibbs are well rated in Scotland and we had run them everywhere.

After the Old Bill let us go the city centre descended into chaos. English lads came from all directions, the firm numbered what must have been close on a thousand with lads from all over. We were again reunited with the Zulus and they told us they'd smashed a pub to bits full of Villa, fair-play. The city centre continued in the same vein, absolute chaos, large numbers of lads were entering bars and just smashing the fuck out of anything and everything. The Old Bill had lost control and the Jocks were coming under fire in a big way. At this point, me and a few of our lot jumped in a black cab and went to the ground because we had tickets. It was a fair few minutes before we could get away from all the mayhem and on our way to Hampden Park. The taxi dropped us off close to the ground and we went into the game. This next bit is hearsay but our lads without tickets numbering 30-40 got away from all of the chaos and got themselves into a bar to watch the game. When England scored, our lot celebrated and the bar quickly turned moody and from what I have been told basically erupted - glasses and bottles were flying everywhere. Our lads fought like fuck alongside some Blackburn lads. During this row our lad Bail' from Great Barr took a glass in the face from a low-life Jock coward. It left a very bad gash needing many stitches. I know it goes on a lot during football fights but this glass/bottle throwing business really does my head in. It's cowardice of the highest order. I have been the victim of this numerous times over the years both at the football and whilst working the door. It gets my goat and Bail' taking what he did spoiled my, and no doubt his, day. Everyone involved in football troubles knows the pitfalls and dangers but seeing that wound turned my stomach. It took the gloss off what was a cracking day. I am reliably informed our lads did themselves proud during that incident. The Blackburn lads were quoted as saying our lads were fucking mental and as game as they come.

After the game, the Old Bill we all over us. They held us all together for what seemed ages. Roughly 15 of our lot managed to get together. We were then bussed into the city centre and dropped off near to Queen Street Station in the city centre where we walked from towards Glasgow Central. Our lot who didn't have tickets had gone to Hamilton in preparation to catch the coach home. The 15 of us entered the side entrance into the station. I was at the back of our lot talking to my pal on the phone and the next thing I knew a Geordie approached me and asked for a hand. Some Jocks were hassling him and he was alone. At this point I was still on the phone then suddenly I was punched from behind. My phone went up in the air and it was again game on. I put four or five really good meaty digs into the first Jock within punching distance. He went down like a ton of shit and lay across the bottom of the escalator knocked out. Me and the Geordie then came under fire from five or six Jocks. The rest of ours were already nearing the top of the escalators when the fight started. On reaching the top they came charging back down the stairs but by the time they got to us the incident was over. The Old Bill were on the scene, I had received a fair few digs after the initial punches were thrown but I had got my fair share in and done more damage than they had. Jamie from Nuneaton had also grabbed one by the jacket, dragged him down the stairs and gave him a few slaps so we didn't do badly at all. English OB had us now. They told us to get the fuck out of the area so we left there and went downstairs to the underground part of the station to catch the train to Hamilton. Downstairs we bumped slap bang into some of our good old foes, Wolves including the TV documentary star referred to by our lot as Teflon. At this point, I realised my phone had gone so I went back upstairs to look for it. Luckily the police had it so after proving it was mine I went back downstairs to see that Wolves had gone, along with a few of our lot, on the same train towards Hamilton. We called ahead to our lot in Hamilton to let them know the sketch and that we would follow on the next train. When their train arrived in Hamilton our lot were waiting, but there was no sign of them. Their vans were definitely parked in Hamilton, that's why we were parked there. We had prior notice they were parking there so we did likewise hoping to bump into them. When we arrived on the next train we discovered it had gone off in a local pub with some of our lot and Eamon had been nicked. We waited an hour or so for the rest of our lot to filter in from Glasgow while trying to obtain news of our other lads nicked earlier in Glasgow. We were told they were being held until Monday and straight into court. I didn't envy them.

Once we had gathered all of our lot together we headed for home. It was a quiet, sombre mood on the way home probably due to the fact we had been on a two-day drink and drugs session and everyone was knackered. At roughly 11pm, when we were just south of Manchester on the M6, my phone rang. It was a Wolves bod asking our whereabouts. I told him where we were and asked why they had not called us all day and also where they hid in Hamilton. No reply. I politely told him to fuck off and ended the call. Absolute jokers. But overall a great day with what was one of the best faces-wise Albion firm I had ever travelled with.

Bailey's wound required more than 50 stitches, leaving a hefty scar but he maintains it is par for the course.

Bailey: There were about 30 of us in this pub as we had no tickets for the game and we had to find somewhere with a TV. It was packed and me and my mate, Steve, tossed a coin to see who was going to the bar. He lost so off he went and I went to sit down. I asked this lad if I could sit down near him. He said no but I thought fuck it and sat down anyway. When England scored we all jumped up and a lad in a Russ Abbot wig threw a glass and then it kicked off. I then remember this lad coming from the side and he threw a glass and it caught my face. I didn't realise I'd been cut and after a bit when we were going out, I remember a copper looked away when he saw me and said I needed to go to hospital. As I went outside and the cold air hit me I felt heat on my face and that's when I realised I was bleeding.

I found out my saliva gland had nearly been slashed and I needed 53 stitches on the side of my face. I went for a beer after, covered in blood while waiting to go back home. The barman wouldn't serve me though. It was all over my top, jeans and shoes. I told him I'd had my trouble wasn't after any more I just wanted a drink. He agreed if I went and washed up a bit in the toilets. My missus went mad when I got back and I'll also never forget what my mum said to me as well. She told me she was always proud of me going everywhere to watch England and she told all her friends what I did but "You don't go for football, you go for violence... really you're a Neanderthal." I'll never forget that.

On the coach on the way home, people were saying sorry to me but as far as I am concerned it happens. The more times you're there the more chance you have of something like that happening to you. I had my knuckles battered in during a mad row with Man United, one of the maddest ones I've seen, and a metal plate was put in my hand. It is part of it and worse has happened to others.

Phil E on the pitch at Shrewsbury in 1992 taking a
photo of KJ, fist clenched, Joey and Toby

What was left of the goalposts at Shrewsbury after mass pitch invasion

Section 5 lads drinking on Southsea front 1994
when they clashed with Pompey

Albion and Pompey get to grips on the pitch at Fratton Park 1994

Freethy meets the King, Jeff Astle 13th January 1995

Down at Bournemouth for FA Cup Third Round 1999

Amsterdam after bashing Wolves

Old Trafford August 2002. L-R: Carl C, Stevie Guy and Big Jon

Yew Tree lot at 2006 World Cup in Germany

The Old Guard. L-R: Mickey Rogers, Psycho, Bowie,
Leftie, Frankie F, and the author, Snarka

Young and old – Yew Tree and Section 5 at the Tiger pub August 2008

More youth at Stone Cross pub ahead of a game
against Villa in 2008/9 season

Mugshots of mainly banned lads from part of police intelligence file

Gathering at Blue Gates pub 2008

Job done, L-R: Big Jon, Caroline, Freethy and Snarka

Chapter Thirteen
Loathe Thy Neighbour

Big Jon: Not a lot of organisation went into us playing Blues at theirs in September 1999. Since the early Nineties there had been no real hostilities between us and them, a few incidents had taken place but nothing large scale. A few conversations had taken place about this fixture and the word was simply to meet in the Billiard Hall pub in West Brom, see who and how many turned up and take it from there. On the day, numbers were not too good with a maximum of 80. But, that included a lot of our best faces so what we lacked in numbers didn't matter. The fixture also seemed to get rid of a lot of hangers-on for some reason. We left the Billiard Hall just before 2pm and headed for West Bromwich central tram station and headed to Snow Hill Station in Birmingham. The police were nowhere to be seen so our journey went unnoticed which was strange but we were pleased. Arriving at Snow Hill we expected to be met by some Old Bill but again, strangely enough, we weren't so we headed out across the city through the area around the law courts and down towards Digbeth, a well known Zulu stronghold. Still we went unnoticed which was odd but, as I have mentioned, no real hostility exists between us and the Zulus so maybe the police were a little off-guard.

After a 10-15 minute walk towards St Andrews we came up towards the Forge pub. It was a regular Zulu haunt so we were on our guard and ready for anything. Just as we were by the pub a firm of about 30 Blues, a mix of black and Asian lads, came out of a side street on our right-hand side. We recognised a few well-known faces. Our lot simply went straight into them forcing them back up the street they'd just come from. A few digs were handed out and numerous missiles thrown and these Blues lot disappeared into the distance. During the row they were on their phones obviously to their lads telling them about us. We kept on the move and turned onto Great Barr Street still en route to the ground. As we walked some of the Blues lot we'd just encountered came walking up along side us. I must give it to them, they had some serious front but some of them were a little naïve to say the least. Some of us had a pop at them again and it looked like their front was going to see them severely filled in. We were now near the park at the bottom of Garrison Lane and another Blues pub, the Garrison, is situated just the other side of the park. It looked like the lads inside were aware of us and were starting make their way over to us and it was then the Old Bill surfaced for the first time and in huge numbers. They gathered us all together and held us at the side of the road whilst they got rid of any Blues lads. At this point, I believe we had done more than the vast majority of firms do at Birmingham, not necessarily in a fighting sense. We had arrived in the city with no police interest, walked straight through Digbeth, their stronghold, and faired well in any exchanges thus far. Our activities had obviously spread and during our escort for the rest of the journey to the ground several Blues faces popped up to have a look at us.

Just as we arrived at the visitor's turnstiles, a firm of Blues attempted to have a go at us coming through the passageway just by the bingo hall. They failed and the Old Bill pushed them back and away from us. As we got to the coach park adjacent to our turnstiles, several well-known Blues faces from where I'm from confronted me through the dividing fence. They were asking me what I thought we were doing and we were taking the piss. This was the problem for me regarding this fixture. I was friends with many faces on the Blues side and living where I do makes life difficult if I am involved in any Blues/ Albion incidents. Saying that and despite the respect I have for those Blues faces, at the end of the day I am Albion and when push comes to shove my loyalty is 100% with Albion. This stance has caused me many problems over the years but at the end of the day I will not apologise for where my loyalty lies.

We drew the game 1-1 and afterwards we all said to leave together and stick together. We'd upset a good few on the Blues side and I am sure a little attempt at redemption was on the cards. Out on the main road, it quickly became apparent this was a hostile situation. Loads of lads and fans were milling about and I was immediately confronted by a face I knew from my area. I pointed out that this was not the time or the place and I would speak to him later if he considered we had an issue that needed resolving. We numbered around 60 here. God knows where the rest were because as well as our 80-plus pre-game, there were also plenty of our lads at the game. Maybe the Old Bill had them but either way, we were out on the street surrounded by Blues lads and fans and it was looking moody to say the least.

We made our way away down the hill towards the traffic island adjacent to McDonalds where a well known Blues face approached me giving it loads telling me to come over with them and making references to how big I was. I pointed out we were outnumbered on a massive scale and that if he/they wanted it, we were there and there now so what was the delay or problem? Old Bill was his reply. I said I wasn't daft and pointed out that if I did come with them, how many did they need to kick my head in? I think they were getting more wound up by the minute and our 60 stuck together and gave out as much verbals as we were receiving. One Asian Blues lad was also in amongst our lot, giving it loads. I don't doubt the fact that Blues are a top firm because on their day they are a match for most and better than many but, they also contain many hangers-on and this Asian lad fell into that category. Tony F gave him an almighty back-hander and told him to fuck off, which he did pretty quickly. We were now walking on one side of the road with Blues on the other and it looked like the further we moved down the road, the more likely it was going to erupt. The police were starting to filter in amongst and between us and as we reached the island they completely surrounded us and held us at the side of the road. Blues lads and fans were coming past us in their droves, plenty of banter was going back and forth but the Old Bill had us well and truly surrounded. We were going nowhere during this stand-off.

A Blues lad appeared at the rear of our lot as he'd managed to sneak through a little side street. He had a conversation with Connor, a lad from Oldbury, and instructed him where to go for a row. Connor simply dropped the nut on him and smashed a can of pop over his head. The lad was in a state with his nose spread all over his face and claret everywhere which was highly amusing and again displayed the arrogance and stupidity of some Blues lads. But all that went unnoticed to the Old Bill. When the area had cleared a bit, the police began to escort us towards the city centre but the route was a long one to avoid Digbeth High Street where Blues would be. Whilst being escorted, our phones started ringing. Our other lads, not in the escort, were around Snow Hill Station in the city centre and were involved in a row with a firm of Blues. Our lot faired quite well in this exchange, despite being outnumbered but the Old Bill were quickly on the scene. Eventually we arrived at Snow Hill and the Old Bill led us onto the tram and we left and that was that.

After that day, I had several conversations with my Blues pals and when tempers had calmed down, everything was fine. They gave our lot respect for our efforts. I think if it had gone off on our exit from the ground when we were 60-handed, it would have been very moody due to the massive numbers difference. All I can say is whatever would have happened we would have stood our ground, that I know 100%. I have recently read the Zulu book and I have big respect for the Blues lads who live in my area, they're lads I've grown up with and known for 30-plus years. I have been criticised in certain circles for giving Blues too much respect. I won't apologise for this because, as I have mentioned many times throughout my input in this book, I speak as I find and also speak my mind. CC and Wally are lads in their own right. I do not doubt what they have published and Blues respect country-wide backs up what they have to say. Wally's points in his Rocky Lane court case were certainly food for thought and I take my hat off to him for having the bollocks to take on the Old Bill, prosecution and the judge and get a not guilty. What he did took some extreme bollocks but overall his intelligence won the day.

One point I would like to put across is, this numbers business regarding the Lewisham incident when we met in the mid-Eighties. I hold my hands up because Wally is correct on that score. Blues did not number 150 but they certainly did not number 30 so, I think you need some maths lessons as well son. Also, he made a point about Blues running Albion ragged after the game. Simply not true. If he is referring to the incident in Middlemore Road where Apollo 2000 now stands, then I was there. We backed Blues off down the road first and then Blues did likewise and backed us back up the road as Joseph mentions in his contribution to the book. The Old Bill then intervened and pushed us back and away from the area with a load more of our lot arriving at the time. We have faced both authors during numerous incidents, something they have failed to mention for whatever reason. Only they know but, I can guarantee them one thing, out of all the Midland firms, we would give them their hardest task if it ever came to it. That I know for sure.

* * * * * * *

Rotherham away in November 2001 was one of those strange, funny days where a lot of lads seemed to turn up for no apparent reason. We had no history or problem with Rotherham. Birmingham were playing at Sheffield United which meant they were travelling on the same train routes as us but if anything, a pop at Sheffield was our intention. We travelled up north early doors, numbering 50-60 of mainly older lads with a few youngsters mixed in. The usual suspects were out - Phil, Lynx, Keith, Dougy, Joey, Spenna, Chinda, the Great Barr lads Peachy, Clem, Keron and the Stone Cross lads Cola and Oggy. The journey up to Sheffield was uneventful. There were a mixture of Blues and West Brom fans on the train but it was quiet and to be perfectly honest, normal fans are of no interest whatsoever to us when it comes to trouble. We are not bullies and we do not attack innocents. When we arrived at Sheffield, the station was awash with Old Bill. They held us to the side and then escorted us onto a little local train they had held back for us. Another 20 of our lot, mostly youngsters including Simo and brothers Steve and Gavin were amongst this lot, good lads who are well thought of.

We headed to Rotherham with plenty of phone calls going on between us and more of our lot en route to Sheffield and Rotherham. That's the problem with West Brom. Unfortunately, we never seemed to travel together for some unknown reason.

At Rotherham it was again complete Old Bill overkill. They held us for a time and then escorted us towards a pub they must always put away fans into. This was roughly around midday and over time more of our lot arrived and eventually we started to drift out of this boozer because the police surrounded it. We left in ones and twos with the arrangement that we would meet further up the road in the town centre. This tactic worked and 30 minutes later, a fair few had snuck away. We were close on a 100-strong in another boozer. Phil, Lynx and Chinda went for a scout about and literally bumped straight into Rotherham's firm. They numbered about 40 and were a little lively. To be honest, I don't think they understood how many lads we had up there.

After a little deliberation between the two groups, our lot returned to relay what had been said. But Rotherham had different ideas and followed them. Our lads rounded the corner of a street where a good 100 of us were plotted up in the pub with the locals not far behind them. One of our lads must have made a phone call because the shout went up in the pub and we all piled out as Rotherham rounded the corner with a look of shock across their faces. They faced a good 120 lads and they were off like a shot. We did start to chase them but gave up pretty quickly and the Old Bill were on the scene fairly sharp-ish.

We went back in the pub and the Old Bill surrounded it outside and we were going nowhere. After a while, several coppers came in, including our intelligence officer. They said that we'd have to leave soon and be escorted to the ground. Our copper approached me and asked me what our plans were. He told me to sort our lot out and get everyone in order. I think you can guess my reaction and I told him politely to fuck off. I didn't consider I was in any position to tell any of our lot what to do and I don't have the slightest clue why he thought I was in a position to do so. We had some main faces present and I wasn't interested in giving people orders. They began emptying the pub and about 10 of us stayed out of the way and let them get on with it. All of our lot outside were on the move after a while but we stayed and the Old Bill left us. We had another drink and decided to have a walk up towards the ground. Most of us lot didn't have tickets and several were actually on bans. We moved up by the ground and visited a pub close by but I moved on at this point and went to the game. They stayed in the pubs by the ground and after a while moved back up into the town centre. They were in contact with some of the Rotherham lads because they had exchanged numbers earlier in the day. The beer and white stuff had been flowing all day and those not at the game were at the rowdy stage and were inviting Rotherham to pay them a visit in all the pubs they were in. But Rotherham didn't show up and the local landlords were beginning to lose patience with this small group of our lot. A disagreement led to a pub being smashed up. The lot went apparently, optics, and windows.

When the game finished, which we lost 2-1, the lads at the match moved back up towards the town centre. Our small group of barmy lads were plotted up in a pub out of the way and we all filtered up towards them. After half-an-hour we numbered about 70-80 and Rotherham were not interested in getting anything on so we decided to make a move. When we headed back up to the town centre and station we could see in the distance that some of our lads were involved in a fracas with what looked like local lads and police. As we got nearer it was clear the locals had disappeared and the Old Bill were throwing their weight around but their chins hit the floor when they saw us. They got us all together - our 70-80 and the other 30-40 of our lot involved in this latest disturbance - and escorted us to the station. Our day in Rotherham was now over. At this point I will again repeat what I said earlier. We don't have a problem with Rotherham it was just one of those days when a good few of our older and younger faces showed up for a day. We don't consider we did anything of any note at their place and we don't consider they disgraced themselves in any way either really. They've got some good lads who I've met on England trips. We simply had the numbers and faces and were also organised and in town early doors.

But now the fun began. We were put on the train to Sheffield and obviously Birmingham would be about but we fancied having a pop at Sheffield United. Although as we entered the station, any thoughts of us getting out of it evaporated as it was complete Old Bill overkill, again. It seemed like there were hundreds of plod there and they meant business and weren't taking any nonsense. We were escorted off the train up onto the station walk-way then they forced us down the steps onto the platform that the Birmingham train would stop on. As we came down the stairs we could see the platform was split into two with Birmingham one side and our lot on the other. There were already loads of our lot on the platform before this good 100 of us lot joined them. There was a bit of banter flying back and forth but with the no-nonsense Old Bill presence and the insults getting more serious by the minute, the atmosphere quickly turned nasty. The Old Bill are supposedly there to diffuse any potentially volatile situations but in this instance they were lighting the fuse and it was no surprise when the whole platform erupted into violence. Albion made a determined effort to get to the Birmingham contingent but the Old Bill prevented this happening.

Any thought of an off with Birmingham was quickly forgotten. The trouble was between Albion and the Old Bill. They weren't interested in arresting anyone and their soul intention was to hit anything that moved with their batons and many of our lads suffered. I was fairly near to the front of the action when I noticed Keith, a pal from Cradley, coming under fire from the plod. I moved forward to pull him out of the firing line when I was struck full-blast over the head with a baton. It split my head leaving a serious gash and I was well pissed off so I simply steamed into the Old Bill. I managed to get one good punch in and a few kicks, then all hell broke loose and the Old Bill turned their attentions to me en masse and I received one hell of a beating. Matters were not helped when Cola fell over behind me and I fell over him and the beating was even more intense. Every time I tried to get up they hit me, kidneys, knees, thighs and head, everywhere they could. I was in a bad way. Whilst I was being dealt with, the rest of our lot were having a right go. Missiles were flying everywhere and the Old Bill were coming in for serious punishment. They weren't having it all their own way far from it but, eventually after one hell of a ding-dong, order was restored. We were forced onto the waiting train and that was it.

The vast majority of the Birmingham contingent didn't get on the train and to be honest I couldn't blame them. We were lawless that day. I managed to clean myself up a bit on the journey home but my head was bleeding and I needed stitches and my clothes were in a right state. Every limb and joint ached as our lot had a heated debate about what had happened. The general feeling was one of disbelief in that only one of our lot had been nicked, which was Keith, meaning my rescue attempt was in vein anyway. The journey home was a laugh as we talked about what had gone on and when we reached New Street my day was over. I jumped on a local train home but about 60-70 of our lot decided to visit the Trocadero pub in Birmingham city centre which is a Villa pub. They stayed in there for quite a good while but nothing occurred.

So, with the day over and despite a severe beating and ruining £600 - £700 worth of clothes, I enjoyed it a great deal. It was a laugh and if the Old Bill took that stance every week with regards to giving out beatings rather than arrests and prison sentences, football would still be a cracking day out.

* * * * * * *

For Villa at theirs in December 2002 the usual suspects organised proceedings. Phil, Chinda and me did our homework and certainly put in a lot of effort in for this one.

Villa is my derby game rather than Wolves. A split exists between our fans/lads as to who they see as our local rivals. The Black Country folk see Wolves as our rivals in the main, the rest simply hate Villa. The week before this fixture Villa were playing Newcastle at home and myself and a couple of other lads took the opportunity to have a drive down Aston and the surrounding areas to have a look what was what and who was where. It was quickly apparent that the areas where Villa's lads frequented were swarming with Old Bill. If you talk to any Villa lad the remark is always the same "Come to the Lichfield Road". We oblige and it was swarming with plod plus, the fact the other boozer they frequented, known as the Addy, is right next to Queens Road police station - one of the biggest police stations in Birmingham! All rather amusing I think.

We spent a good two hours having a look around, even checking the city centre and our conclusion was that if we took it to them the Old Bill would be all over it before it started - that was if we even managed to get anywhere near the Lichfield Road. Before being picked up, bearing in mind this was a big game, I estimated we would have around 300 lads out with probably more milling around as well. I suggest you have very little or no chance of getting very far with those numbers involved. At first, we looked at a pub in Newtown called the Shareholders, which is within striking distance of the Lichfield Road. After looking at the route between there and the Lichfield Road we knew we had no chance of getting through with no Old Bill interest. It was patrolled on a regular basis so, that was a no-no early on. We eventually decided on a pub in Perry Barr called the Calthorpe. It's roughly a mile to the ground and we thought we could all meet in separate areas and pubs and eventually converge at the Calthorpe with no police interest whatsoever. We checked the pub out. It had two fairly big rooms and the management and bar staff were a mixture of Albion and Villa fans so job was a good one. We had it all sorted from our point of view. We thought that if we all got plotted up early doors, we could keep it quiet and eventually try to get Villa up towards us.

The plans went into over-drive and in the week leading up to the game, many phone calls went to all the different groups that make up Albion's firm. Everyone agreed on what we had sorted out and the arrangements were finalised. On the morning of the game me and the Bearwood, Oldbury, Rowley, Nuneaton, Quinton and Selly Oak lads met in the Grove pub, roughly half-a-mile from the Calthorpe. It was early doors but there were plenty of lads milling about and no Old Bill. The signs were it was going to be a good day. Phones were buzzing and the plan was in motion and at around midday, everyone started to filter towards the Calthorpe. We were all keeping our whereabouts quiet for the time being to keep Old Bill interest away from us. An hour later, we had between 150 and 200 lads at the Calthorpe, still with no police present. Faces present included lads from the areas already mentioned plus Blackheath, Cradley Heath, Tipton, Whiteheath, Stourbridge, Kidderminster, Dudley, Wednesbury, Smethwick, Tividale and many areas of West Brom. There was also a strong contingent from Stone Cross and a good showing from Yew Tree estate. This fixture always brings out the well respected older faces. We had good numbers with quality lads out, who were ready for anything that came our way. Then the phone calls started between us and Villa. The Lichfield Road line from them was trotted out, amusingly enough. We put our point in early "We are in Perry Barr with no Old Bill whatsoever, make your way up and we will meet you on the way". Simple as that. I don't think we could have done any more. Our scouts reported Villa were surrounded by Old Bill, no shock there.

At 2pm we had at least 250 lads at the Calthorpe and the phones were in meltdown. Shortly after that, one of our lads had a phone call from a Villa friend of his. He and numerous Villa were in the Little Crown pub, a short distance from where we were. His cockyness was highly amusing, little did he know we had a massive firm within a five minute walk of where he and his pals were. The call went up and we were on the move. We had a van parked close by with a whole host of tools and some very meaty flares stashed in it. We left this alone for the time being and made our way to the main Walsall Road and to the pub where Villa had called us from. I was more or less in the middle of our lot and the walk was five minutes if that.

As we reached the main road and rounded the island, the scene in front of us was one of chaos. The pub was under heavy attack. Our lot that first arrived on the scene said Villa, numbering 40-50, had come out of the pub at first but sheer numbers forced them back with some of them receiving a good few slaps before managing to get back inside. With our entire firm now on the scene, the pub was literally ripped to bits.

Fair-play to some of the Villa lot, they were doing their best to hold the doors. I along with a few others attacked the door on the other side of the pub. The Villa in the doorway were throwing missiles out of the door and I caught a glass in the side of the face which gashed my face and ear. We smashed whoever was in the doorway and one of our lads lifted the metal interior of a bin out of its holder to smash through the windows. When its contents covered a load of our lot it stank, it was blood, guts and whatever else from a butcher shop close by. Dirty bastards, the smell clung to everyone for the rest of the day. The pub had been ripped to bits and the occupants defeated. We had the numbers advantage but that was not our problem and after all, they made the phone call. How they regretted that, I bet.

The sirens were now coming from every direction, the Old Bill were all over us pretty quickly. The West Brom intelligence were in attendance and getting amongst us. I think they were pissed off we had given them the slip. They were totally clueless as to where we were and how we had got to Perry Barr in such numbers without being noticed - 1-0 to us on all counts. They held us all a short distance away from the scene of the trouble. I was one of the last to leave the scene because the Old Bill had collared Bail'. I helped him out and got him away from them saying I'd look after him just to get him away. We joined our lot round the corner when low and behold I am nicked. A police dog was set on my pal so we got it off and a plod gave me a mouthful of abuse so I returned fire. Not clever after what had just occurred and as I say, I was nicked and put in the van with another one of our lads from Derby. Our lot were then escorted towards the ground and the van we were in followed the them down towards the ground. I was arguing with the plod that had nicked me for the entire journey. His threats of court action were met with insults from me. He was talking bollocks. My point was that he had insulted me and I returned in kind, fairs fair in my book and eventually, he softened in his approach.

As we arrived at Witton Island, our main escort had gone but then another firm of our lot, including our main face, J, strolled past - another quality firm of 20 to 30 present. At the ground, the plod that nicked me changed his mind about court action, admittedly I had relented a bit in my stance and we had settled our differences in the main. He cautioned me, relieved me of my match ticket and said that if he saw me again that day I would be done without hesitation. Lucky escape and our lad from Derby was also freed with the same treatment minus his ticket as well. I made a call to some of my pals who didn't have tickets. They had moved back up towards Handsworth and were in the Endwood pub so I walked back up towards Perry Barr and jumped on a bus to meet them. Tony and Jamie, our lads from Nuneaton, said they had seen Villa leaving the Little Crown after our lot were escorted away. They numbered 40-50 with some well known older faces present. But after the event, Villa claimed there was no one present on their side. We know different, as does the fool that made that fateful call. We numbered 10-15 in the Endwood and calls were being made between our lot in the game and in several pubs in the area. We planned to let

it die down after the match and then take it to Villa in their pubs in the
city centre.

The game ended in a 2-1 defeat for us and not long after we moved
from the pub in Handsworth into the city centre. We converged on
Yates's in Corporation Street by the law courts. We numbered between
25 to 30 but more of our lot were drifting in from the game. The Square
Peg pub was a short distance from where we were plotted up which
was one of Villa's drinking holes. We planned to land on it and smash
anything and anyone who wanted it. Our numbers continued to grow
and at roughly 6.30pm we decided to move up there. We were 50-60
handed at this stage with more on the way. Most of our lot at the game
had drifted back to their own areas unaware anything was building
up in the city centre. We just went with what we had and there were
some good faces out. We approached their pub and discovered that
Villa weren't inside so we went in and got ourselves comfy and had a
drink. This was a piss take already so we had to wait to see what was
coming next. Our numbers continued to grow and a good group from
Great Barr appeared. The firm was getting better by the minute. Phone
calls were made to Villa as soon as we arrived and continued for about
an hour. Yes, it took them that long to finally arrive. Some of our lot got
fed up with waiting and simply drifted away during the hour we spent
in the pub. Villa sent numerous scouts to the pub while we waited
and my guess is they simply waited until our numbers decreased
sufficiently enough in their opinion before having a pop at us. They
tried this tactic after an FA Cup match at Villa Park in 1996 when, after
the game, we moved back into the city centre and filled several pubs,
one being the Wellington. They watched our lot gradually drift away
until they thought enough had gone and they attacked. About 20 of
our lot remained but Villa failed miserably and made complete fools
of themselves.

When Villa finally made an appearance this time we numbered
roughly 40. They were about the same number, fronted by a half-caste
lad. I don't think they realised how many we had present because it's a
big pub. Our lot came from all directions and the 40 Villa were simply
smashed out of the pub. We came out of the pub, onto the side of the
road and Villa ran in all directions followed by some of our lot. They
had taken some casualties who had received a good kicking. Then
another firm of Villa came through the pub in the direction of where
we had exited from. They threw missiles at us which we returned with
interest - a big bar stool came flying out so I picked it up and gave a few

of them a good whack with it. These Villa seemed a tad naïve. A few of them came in amongst us telling their pals inside the pub to get outside with them. These fools were severely filled in. One even pleaded to be left alone saying "I'm sorry" repeatedly. Very amusing. Some of our lot chased some Villa as far as one of their other pubs called the Trocadero. They were cornered and set for a good hiding when they again pleaded to be left alone because they were friends with some of our lot from Cradley. Chinda and Eamon, amongst others, gave them the benefit of the doubt and gave them a pass out, lucky for them.

Some fighting then continued in the road at the rear of Rackham's department store. I was there for this and we had a good toe-to-toe with similar numbers for a good five minutes. We did some damage here in dishing out some punishment. I caught one with probably one of the best punches I have ever thrown. The geezer was sparked out before he hit the ground. The half-caste lad fronting the Villa firm earlier was game but he had very little back up and in the end, one of our lads, Doug, gave him a good few slaps and he joined the rest of his lot backing off at a rapid rate. Now the job was done with this lot, we moved back down towards the Square Peg. We encountered a few more Villa en route and gave them a slap. Moving further down towards the pub, we encountered what we thought was another little firm of Villa. We went straight into them and low and behold they were plain clothes Old Bill.

Eamon and Doug were nicked and the other eight to10 of us managed to do a sharp exit and get away.

Chinda was cornered by the Old Bill but he managed to blag them that he was in the pub with his missus when all hell had broken loose and he had lost her in the chaos. We all met back up in Colmore Row and decided our best bet was to get out of there. We considered we'd achieved what we had come for and really taken the piss.

Eamon and Dougy were charged with assault for their encounter with the coppers, amongst other things, and eventually had to go to court. CCTV footage clearly showed Villa en-route to the pub picking up bricks and anything they could throw. It also clearly showed exactly what had happened and how many were involved. Villa were run all over the place and a fair few of them received a good beating. The excuses afterwards and ever since really have been downright pathetic and laughable.

If a firm came into West Brom and plotted up in one of our pubs, it would take us minutes to get there, not the hour they took. We could do no more on that day in my opinion. We were out early with no Old Bill whatsoever and, after an invite we did the business with superior numbers and again later in the evening, 40 of us had gone into their back yard and taken the piss.

Eamon and Dougy had a decent result in court and received a big fine and numerous other punishments. To be honest, I thought we were all for it because the CCTV coverage is all over the place in that area but, surprisingly nothing more ever came of it. A great result all round. Fair-play and respect to the 40 lads, young and old, present at the Square Peg incident. We stood together and did the business, despite the bullshit and excuses. We are safe in knowledge about what happened and who did what. Villa to this day have never returned the favour and come anywhere near our town or where we drink apart from a very futile effort in Smethwick once when they were again caught out and done.

PART SIX

Chapter Fourteen
The Premiership Years

Tony: Wolves had a lead of 11 points going into the run-in and looked odds-on to gain promotion at the end of the 2001/2 season. But, with an amazing sequence of results and West Brom's final away win at Bradford City we only had to win our final game at home against Crystal Palace and we would be in the Premiership after a 17-year break from top flight football. But if we lost or drew and they won, they would go up.

On the morning of the game, a lot of our lads met up at the Stone Cross pub for our annual St George's Day march which at the time was deemed illegal by the authorities. There were probably 300-plus out at the time - unlike the 10,000-odd we get now it's legal and officially recognised. As we made our way to Carters Green, all the talk was of the forthcoming game. People were worried, nervous and just dying for it to come. It was very exciting and tense, everyone was begging for tickets with people even up by the ground offering silly money for their tickets. Quite a few were successful I might add. It was one of the first times I can remember the ground being absolutely chocker half-an-hour before kick off. Everyone was going ballistic, screaming and singing untold amount of obscenities towards our most hated enemies during our anthem The Liquidator - something else Wolves fans bullshit everyone about saying it's theirs. Liars. The teams came out to an unbelievable reception and we were off but, within five minutes Wolves were one up at Sheffield Wednesday. Nerves were jangling to say the least but I've never heard a ground so noisy. It was non-stop and it obviously worked because on 17 minutes, Big Dave put us one up. I really can't put into words how I and everyone felt and acted. Only people there that day would understand. It was a feeling of euphoria, mania, total mayhem and happiness. Everyone was just hugging and jumping up and down, the noise was deafening.

In the final minutes news came back that the shite were losing 2-1 and to top it all off our legend Bob Taylor banged in the second. You can imagine the chaotic scenes that followed when the final whistle blew as everyone swarmed onto the pitch.

The Old Bill never even bothered to stop them. The scenes were surreal. Every blade of grass was covered by the happiest fans. Sweeter still, was the fact that we knew Albion had fucked them wankers up from Dingle-hampton. They'll never forget it, nor will we. Ha ha. After what seemed like an eternity people started to leave the ground it was a mass party all the way back to West Brom. Car horns were constantly going off, roads were full of drunken Albion fans up lampposts, on top of cars, bus shelters, all singing, screaming and everyone hugging everyone. It really is hard to explain just how incredible the scenes were but they are memories that stay with you forever.

However, word kept coming via the phones during the day that the "mighty Wolves" were paying us a visit. So most of the lads moved further into the middle of the town but, as it got later it was pretty obvious these were again idle threats. As you can imagine on a day such as this, Albion's firm was huge with hundreds of young and old out and as the night got nearer and nearer and the beer flowed, the police decided it was time to move people on. But as always, they started to get heavy-handed. Our firm got pissed off with them and inevitably the town exploded. Glasses, bottles, bricks, anything they could lay their hands on was thrown at them as the kicks and punches went on. But as the time went on with us driving them back and vice versa, the police eventually got on top. Of course, as the police started to struggle, out came the cameras as so often is the case. They start it to get what they want, a name to the faces. It all ended with a load of jail sentences and bans again. I'll give the Old Bill up West Brom their due as nicking and banning lads for next to fuck all has always been their speciality. So, as usual a great day was spoilt by the over exuberance of our police and again Wolves didn't turn up but, would probably tell everyone they did.

* * * * * * *

Big Jon: Prior to our first season in the Premiership, numerous debates had taken place between many of our well known faces in relation to where we should meet and drink to stay one step ahead of the Old Bill. We needed somewhere where we could meet up without any interest from them. West Bromwich town centre had become increasingly covered by CCTV and the police were fully aware of our movements at other venues not covered by cameras. Tony Freeth had mentioned many times about us reverting back to old times and drinking in Smethwick at the Blue Gates pub. This massive pub was well known to a whole host of football firms as many rows had occurred in the area in years gone by, though not in recent times. It was a good idea as far as quite a few people were concerned but putting it into practice would be interesting because some of our lot are stubborn so-and-sos at the best of times. A lot of our lot are loyal to West Bromwich as a town and like to stop in that area and move nowhere else. Man City was one of the first home games in Premiership and we tested the water and arrangements were made to meet in the Blue Gates.

I left my house which is a few miles away from Smethwick at about midday and almost immediately when I turned my phone on, I received a call from a very well known Birmingham face that I was on friendly terms with. Man City were in Birmingham drinking with these Birmingham lads because they too were also on friendly terms. The point of the call was to ask our whereabouts. I don't like to give out information of that nature out unless I'm with everyone else, a point I put across to my Birmingham friend so I told him I'd call him back when I knew more. Entering the Blue Gates I was pleasantly surprised. It was just afternoon and plenty of faces were out, we numbered at least 100 with more arriving all the time. I told our faces about the phone call it was agreed I was to call my pal back to tell him to instruct Man City to come to Smethwick via train from New Street and we would be waiting here for them. He asked how many were there of us. "Plenty, with more arriving on a regular basis", I replied and it was left at that.

A little bit of history existed between City. The previous season they had shown up in West Brom town centre in dribs and drabs and were told to leave before they were filled in. This obviously annoyed them and a little later on the main road, close to the ground, some of them came seriously unstuck. I was involved in this, helping out an Albion lad from Blackheath who was being picked on by the Man City group who were instructed to leave the town centre pub earlier...? Without thinking, me and Big Jim got off a bus in the traffic to help the lad out. We went in like a bull in a china shop without realising how many Man City were around. I received some punishment here. After initially giving out a good smack, I came under fire from behind from several lads and I was also hit with a golf club that had been cut off and shortened at the handle. It was painful and left a nasty gash on the side of my head. Luckily Cola, Oggy, Ash and a few other faces were approaching and they steamed in like good-uns. Man City were smacked everywhere and I gained some revenge for my little slapping. Because of the traffic, the Old Bill were hampered in their efforts in getting to the trouble so when they arrived Man City were either on the floor or they had run off. A lot of our lot had melted into the crowd but unfortunately for me, on this day I chose to wear a bright red Lacoste T-Shirt. The plod picked me out and pulled me to one side. They were trying to gather information about the fight from burger vans in the area but this proved to be fruitless. I'd had a lucky escape and they let me go on my way after a short time.

I assume that that group of Man City were faces within their firm because that incident was the obvious reason for their efforts this time around. I rate Man City. I like the football club and its loyal fans so I have no problem with them really and on this day they did exactly what they said they was going to do and turned up in Smethwick at roughly 2pm. We had well over 200 lads out when they arrived and we were confident we were would be okay whatever happened. When word came that they had arrived, we discovered that half of West Midlands Police were also with them after presumably following them from New Street. So this meant game over for the time being and we watched from the pub as the police escorted them up the hill towards the ground. They numbered 100-150 so they would have been well outnumbered for a start. As all this unfolded, the police had no idea whatsoever that close on 250 Albion lads were in close proximity to where Man City had got off the local train. The route to the ground from the station is separated from where we were by a big dual carriageway and Smethwick High Street so our presence went undetected which was a bonus for future plans/games.

At roughly 2.30pm we left the pub and started our walk to the ground. Our numbers had grown a little further still so the walk up was an impressive sight. We didn't encountered anybody en-route to the ground but when we were close to the ground the look on the faces of the Old Bill was one to behold. They were scratching their heads wondering where the hell we had come from. A job well done by our lot.

After the game a fair few of us ventured off back down to the Blue Gates. Nothing happened in and around the ground so it was blatantly obvious the Old Bill had Man City well sewn up. A fair few of our lot drifted away from the pub because it looked as though it was day over and nothing was going to kick off. It was getting on for 7pm when we had a frenzied phone call from Kendo who was in West Bromwich town centre. About 40 to 50 Man City had landed up there and it was going off with our locals who weren't really football lads. I was in one of my vans so a few of us jumped in and shot off up there. It's nearly two miles away from Smethwick and others jumped in taxis. When we got there, City were on the High Street near the Anchor pub and they had Old Bill round them. We jumped out of the van and confronted them. The police forced us back as more of our lot arrived in the cabs so we got together and made an effort to cut around another part of the town and attack them whilst they were getting escorted. This worked although the Old Bill were present.

We had a good go at them and missiles were flying everywhere. No real punches were thrown at this stage they just fronted us and pushed forward at us and we stood our ground. The police continued to push us back and keep them together. At this stage we were at stalemate so again we tried the tactic of cutting around the town to get at them and again it worked. We went into them on a car park at the side of a bar called Busby's. Punches were thrown here and a big Man City lad was hit on the head with a massive bolder from one of our lot, splitting his head from front to back. The Old Bill actually drove in amongst us in cars to try to disperse us but it didn't work and they were losing control. Carl C gave a Man City lad a good few digs and I put one on the floor. We were pushing forward and Man City were starting to flap. They wouldn't come into us and seemed happy to hang back behind the Old Bill. Some of them were game but they got digs and injuries mentioned above. The Old Bill pushed us back and away again so we then moved further around the town and had another go.

Man City could not fault our lot who had arrived from Smethwick because, although outnumbered, we went into them numerous times despite a big Old Bill presence. I think they thought by turning up unannounced it was job done but we had other ideas. Again we fronted Man City but the majority of them seemed happy to stay behind the Old Bill and they were actually singing songs at this stage, very strange. We managed to get a few more digs in and then for the final time the Old Bill forced us back. They had more numbers present now and it seemed if we did not leave the scene arrests would be imminent. But, fair-play to Man City for turning up when and where they did. It seems a little strange that despite knowing we no longer drank in the town they turned up there. They knew we were in Smethwick and if they had turned up there the Old Bill presence was nil and we could have had a serious off. As I say, strange.

Apparently these Man City did not have tickets for the game and the police simply shunted them away from the ground. They had obviously moved offside for a drink, totally undetected and moved into the town later when it was all quiet so fair-play for their efforts. They were doing fairly well until we arrived on the scene. Luckily nobody on our side was nicked. It maybe gave our lot a reminder to stick together after games more but over the years that's the way things happened. When it got to a stage where everyone considered it was day over, lads started to disperse and move back to their areas. Nobody really stayed around the town long into the night because to be honest, despite my loyalty to the football club and the town the night life is not up to much.

* * * * * * *

After the events at our place, the general consensus for the return game in Manchester was that we would travel there in massive numbers and really have a go at City. It was talked about for months and we planned to catch an early train north, before 9am, get off in Stockport and catch buses into Manchester. In the week leading up to the game, the phones were in meltdown and it looked very promising regarding who was travelling and the numbers involved but, on the morning of the game the promising part went out of the window. As I have mentioned, I feel honesty is the best way and maybe it's just me and my loyalty stretches too far but, Man City coming firm-handed firstly to Smethwick and then West Bromwich meant they had laid down a challenge to us and we had no excuse whatsoever for not returning the favour. Before the game, I was confident we would have numbers in the region of 300 to 400 because for big Midland derbies we can pull well in excess of that and it seemed everybody was up for this one. But at New Street, it was clearly obvious we had nowhere near those numbers. We had 60 or 70 which in my opinion was pathetic. That's no blight against the lads present because there was some quality faces out - a good contingent from Stone Cross and Yew Tree and the usual suspects including Chinda, Dougy with some Great Barr lads and Ox and Mike. I felt rather embarrassed though because during many phone calls in the previous week I had guaranteed lads regarding who and how many were travelling.

We headed north and some more lads joined the train at Wolverhampton - Steve B and other Whiteheath lads – so things were improving slightly as we now numbered about 80. At Stockport we left the station in search of a pub that was open.

It was barely 10.30am but we did manage to find somewhere and we all settled down for an early morning drink. Many phone calls were coming in from other lads en route to Manchester/Stockport but I couldn't understand that despite all the arrangements made previously, people had not turned up. It was shoddy to say the least but at this early stage nothing was lost and we still had time to get everyone together in Manchester. A few more of our lads arrived in Stockport, some had travelled up in cars - Spenna and Co were amongst these - so our numbers were gradually growing.

After a while, to our severe distaste it became blatantly obvious either the manager or doormen from the pub we were in had phoned the Old Bill as they appeared outside. This was a severe pain in the arse because all of our planning had gone out of the window and we were going nowhere without any Old Bill interest. We decided the best bet was to get outside the pub and try to catch buses and taxis into Manchester.

On leaving the pub the Old Bill pushed us up towards the bus stops where eventually two stopped and we all jumped on hopeful we would be able to give them the slip en route to Manchester but, they had other plans. They pulled the buses over and cleared them of any other passengers and then escorted us into Manchester. This was a huge disappointment because 40 of our lot were already plotted up in a Manchester pub so our arranged meet with them had gone out of the window.

The journey into Manchester took ages they kept stopping the buses, holding us and then moving on a little further, aiming to delay our arrival at Maine Road as much as possible. We eventually arrived and they stopped the buses in a little side road opposite the away turnstiles. They told everyone that once off the bus we would all be searched, photos taken and our details recorded and checked. This resulted in weapons being dropped and hidden on the buses out of sight of the

Old Bill. It was like a hardware shop with knives, knuckledusters, CS gas, flares the lot getting left.

I bet the Old Bill were well shocked when they found that lot. We meant business that day but were now short of our weapons of mass destruction. We were all searched and checked out and then forced into the ground.

We had a big following that day. The usual away end and a temporary stand in the corner there, over 4,000 fans and, also by now plenty of lads who weren't with us in Stockport or with the other 40 lads in Manchester city centre. The plan was to get together after the game and walk towards the city centre and we would also make an attempt to get at Man City's pubs if we had a chance. The game ended in a 2-1 win for us and we all left the ground in good spirits. As soon as we exited the ground, the Old Bill were all over us. One of our football intelligence officers approached and told me to get in with the group held at the side or I would be nicked. I had little choice obviously. Some lads did manage to escape and had a few scuffles en route to the city centre but we were held for a good 20 minutes before the escort began. We numbered in the region of 150 and our walk was long and tedious. The Old Bill were delaying us as much as they could again for some reason. Eventually we arrived at the station and the Birmingham train was on the platform. We were shoved towards the train some of our lads were already on the platform as we arrived but it was day over really. There were big numbers of our lot on the train and we headed back south, glad that we had won the game but disappointed that our intention of having a go at Man City had not come to fruition.

I was disappointed that despite weeks of planning and people saying that they were coming, many did not show up. We did have loads of lads in the game but if anything had occurred early doors, they wouldn't have been around. Plus, the Old Bill had us sewn up in Stockport anyway. Maybe we should have moved into Manchester by bus as soon as we arrived in Stockport but we'll never know and it's pointless harping on about it now. On the train our lads were mostly in the two rear carriages of the train with the buffet car in between and the Old Bill took great joy in instructing it to close. This was also pointless but obviously they had to justify their overtime payments. After it shut the Old Bill disappeared up the other end of the train, apparently some other football fans were at that end but we don't know who. I was walking past the door of the buffet when out of curiosity I tried the door handle. It opened and with no one in there, I stuffed my pockets full of little spirits bottles and filled my arms with as many cans as I could carry. I came out of the buffet and announced it was open and that everything was free. The place was swamped and cleared out in no time. We sank all the beer and spirits and ate everything in sight even going as far as using the microwave to heat the burgers up. It was a cracking piss take, all thanks to the British Transport Police – fair-play to you lads, we enjoyed your hospitality to the maximum. When everyone had had their fill, the carriage developed into a chaotic food fight which was hilarious and when we got to Wolverhampton, it looked like a bomb had gone off in the two carriages.

Around 60 to70 got off there including me. It was unplanned, just a spur of the moment thing and as we left the station we were approached by a few Old Bill asking who we were. Naturally, our reply was "Wolves", and we made our way across the bridge towards the town centre. We checked the first pub, the Albert, nobody in so we carried on into the town and next up was O'Neils and we settled down for a drink. Some of our lot made calls to their Wolves contacts to let them know we were around but the Old Bill we'd encountered at the station had wised up and realised who we were so they along with many other old bill soon surrounded the pub. So yet again our fun was spoilt by the Old Bill and it was game over. Our continued consumption of drinks was really pissing them and off after a while they came in to let us know that shortly we would have to leave and be escorted to the tram station. If we didn't comply we'd be forcibly removed and arrested. After more delay tactics we were out onto the street and escorted to the tram station where we departed on our way home, day over once again.

Chapter Fifteen
Red Devils and Bluebirds

*A*s well as City, the lads were to face the other side of Manchester as West Brom continued their run in the Premiership. After some lads came unstuck in Manchester before the match on the opening day of the season, there were more than 100 out for the return fixture at the Hawthorns. Big Jon, Cola and Chinda recount events with Man United and subsequent clashes with Cardiff at the home and away fixtures in the 2003/4 season when West Brom dropped back down to Division One.

Cola, as previously mentioned, is well known lad who started getting involved in the scene from about 1985, aged about 16 or 17. He first knew the Great Barr lads - Eamon, Peachy, Bailey and Clem - who were slightly older but as already said, their reputation preceded them. Chinda was one of many lads who became part of the firm as a teenager in the Nineties as the rave scene took hold and pulled lads away from the terraces marking a dramatic change in the hooligan scene. He has been banned from attending matches three times and is currently serving a seven year ban.

Chinda: Man United at ours was a big draw so loads were out. We'd played them in the first game of the 2002/3 season and people got clattered and all sorts in Manchester before the game. They mistook a "Yam Yam" aeroplane chant that West Brom fans do, and Blues sometimes do to us, as banter for a Munich dig and there was a nasty vibe. The younger lot split up and had a row with them on the Metro tram service in Manchester before the game. The Albion youth got a bit of a kicking actually. When they came to ours in January 2003 we were all in the Blue Gates in Smethwick about 10-11am. We heard there were loads of them in West Brom so we all set off to find them but the Old Bill were all around us so there wasn't much we could do really. They were in the Billiard Hall, about 100-150 of them, which was fair-play to them as they got there early, typical them, and took us by surprise. The phones were all going when we heard where they were and it was hectic. People were saying lets attack the pub but you've got to use your head with cameras watching and all that. We went to a few pubs and about 1.30pm and we got everyone to go up to the Lewisham and the Sportsman on the High Street towards the ground. The pubs were packed. We had some spotters waiting outside the Billiard Hall and they stayed in there until about 2.30pm, then we were told they were leaving so everyone got ready. I told people to sit tight and wait a bit.

We sent one of our lads to go and mingle in with them until they jumped on the Metro tram, which they had to use to get up nearer to the ground which was where we were. It's only about a two minute journey to the Lewisham and the tram station is about 100-200 yards from the pub. So about 150 of us went down to meet them by the station. The Old Bill didn't have a clue what was happening, there was only once cop car by the pub. The tram stopped about 30 yards before the station and we said to them "How about it then?" But they said they didn't really fancy it. We all had bricks and bottles and when the tram moved in nearer we attacked it putting the windows through. We were on the phones to one of their lads all day and he said one of them was blinded, but don't know how true that was. We went mad and I'd say they had a good minute to get off and get into it but they didn't come out and they had the opportunity. We piled onto the station and went straight into them trying to drag them out but they weren't having it. The Old Bill eventually cottoned on and appeared so we had to move. You get into someone's town so early and have a chance to have the row and they don't come out of the tram which was disappointing as there was no police about.

As we approached the ground, over the road from the Brummie End, we saw a coach-load of Man United, possibly Cockney Reds, and everybody just went in and attacked them. The Old Bill were in riot gear and were clobbering everyone and four or five of us got nicked, they were more into hitting us really. Even normal fans, shirters whatever, had a go at them too because of what happened before at Old Trafford. As I said, we exchanged phone calls all day with them and after the game they'd got to Blue Gates early, about 40 of them and only a few Albion were there but they had it off and it was on top. We heard they said it was a good row. There were about 20 Albion lads there including Joey, Toby, Peachy, Phil, Chalky and Marsh – we heard they said Peachy looked like Cantona. There was a good 150 Albion walking to the pub and missed the row by minutes really.

Man United do what they say they're going to do and turn up if they say they will. Someone also said Wolves were around which was mad but it was just rumours, happens all the time amongst our lot. One amusing story we heard is that Wolves told Man United to go to the Billiard Hall in West Brom which is funny as they have never been there themselves.

* * * * * * *

Cola: When Man United came to ours around 2004, about 15 of us including me, Freethy, Amber and Pacey went to West Brom on the tram and walked up to the ground. We saw this guy in a Stone Island trench coat, which must have been worth about £500, with a couple of mates. He had a cockney accent and they seemed like lads, singing United songs and acting invincible and that, but as we got nearer one of us just suddenly clocked him and knocked him off his feet. The only thing we regret is not taking his coat - could have got a few hundred quid for that.

We walked on to Middlemore Road which is where the coaches/ visiting fans come in and Albion aren't allowed to go down there but we had managed to get through. We must have been on a suicide mission, all pumped up. We carried on walking and hit random fans walking past, just taking pot shots really. By the time we got to the top of a hill by Apollo 2000, the ones we'd hit must have got together and thought "Hang on. There are only 15 of them". We saw about 30 of them behind us and no Old Bill at all so it just went off. We stood our ground and only time we backed off was when we heard the sirens and the coppers were coming. We made a good account of ourselves then.

All their lads were dressed in Stone Island or whatever and I remember one old boy, unfazed by it all who just walked diagonally through them to us while it was going on. He had a red coat on and big hair and looked like SuperTed. He started fronting us and it was like Queensbury Rules boxing as he put his fists right up and started dancing round us. One lad with us, Pacey, was all covered up like a proper hoolie, hood up and all that, all you could see was his eyes and he was bouncing about in front of the bloke with his fists up shouting "C'maaaann!" It was so funny to see. The old guy got clocked in the end though.

* * * * * * *

Chinda: There was a bit of build up for the mid-week game at Cardiff in November 2003. Some took the day off and about three minibuses and a few cars went. About 50 of us met in a pub Newport and we were having phone calls from lads saying they were on their way down. In the end, about 5pm, Phil said fuck everybody else, let's go. So we got on the motorway for Cardiff and got there about 5.45pm. People got dropped off and went in to the main street, into the Australian Bar which was massive but, they thought if Cardiff came, it would be better to be in a smaller pub so they went over the road to Sam's bar. Jon and me were driving and we parked the vans and as we came back into town we saw them coming and attack the bar. About 20 to 25 Cardiff appeared and our lads, about 50 to 60, went out and slapped a few and chased them off. The Old Bill turned up - our intelligence coppers - and they were shocked big time to see us and what had happened. While all this was going on, we were getting calls about the others on their way, about 20-odd were just up the road but they'd missed it. The police surrounded the bar and wouldn't let anyone go anywhere so we stayed. They told us they were going to take us out in an escort, us lot and the other 20.

In the ground, there were a lot more lads who were trying to pull down the fences to get to Cardiff – an example of people going to matches separately as we only saw them inside and they missed the action. It wasn't long after England won the rugby World Cup so it was all lads singing "Sweet Chariot" and they were singing anti-English stuff, just banter really. Afterwards, loads tried to get out early but the Old Bill stopped us. There were hundreds of us which was something I've not seen at an away game in years. The Old Bill were having none of it so we fought them for about 15 minutes. It was chaos for a bit, we were just steaming straight into them.

They kept us in for about 20 minutes and after that, the cops escorted us out and dispersed everyone. We were disappointed after the game as we thought Cardiff would be waiting around. We had some really good lads out that day.

Big Jon: I got nabbed by the cops straight away outside and they said to leave or get nicked. A load of our lot got together and started walking back the way the cops had escorted them earlier. I was in the van, I drove up and followed them and the cops just stopped them at the side of the road and told them to get in the vans or they would be nicked. There was a coach full of our older lot - a good 40 or 50 - and Cardiff threw a brick at the coach. They pulled the coach over and got off and chased them.

I do a bit of business with some older Cardiff lads and they got in touch afterwards and said we did well. Not many bring firms down on a Saturday never mind a mid-week game and we'd made a show.

Chinda: Prior to them coming to us, we'd heard that Cardiff pick a few fixtures a season and come up the night before and we were told by some Albion lads from down there that they were definitely coming up to ours. Not only had we made a show at theirs but some had been to a few Albion games with our lads and seen some trouble with Wolves. It was a night when we had good numbers and had it off with the Old Bill for about 10 minutes, so word spread amongst Cardiff kind of thing.

On the Friday night before the game, the word was Cardiff were around and people were out looking around. A few of us went to the Ridge Acre, a pub cum hotel by the back of the town centre by Great Bridge as we heard a few were staying there.

I went in with a few lads and Keron appeared later with more and some others also turned up. We were looking but didn't see them there though. The next day for the game, we were about half-a-mile from the Ridge Acre looking for them again, driving around there and town and making phone calls. We heard that they were coming up on two coaches to "smash the town up". Everyone was waiting for them but they never turned up in town.

Cola: The build up to the day for some of us started in the Hargate Arms in West Brom. Some of the Albion youth had got Cardiff's numbers so something had been arranged to meet in the Hargate. There'd also been a lot of banter beforehand on the Internet as well. There were about 100 out from all over for a battle between England and Wales. It brought out even the non-footballing lads, just those who are patriotic - like Bill and Carl from Warley, they don't really come out that much but were out for this one. About six Cardiff did come and have a look in the pub then left saying they would come back. But they never did. Time was moving on and there was stuff going on via the phones but by about 2.30pm we left but to avoid going through West Brom town centre we went cross country. We went through back street and parks and all that to avoid the cops. There were about 80 good lads and we went to the Sportsman and Lewisham and met the others.

Chinda: After being unable to find Cardiff, we moved further into town into the Sportsman and the Lewisham about midday. There must have been about 300-400 of us out and a lot of the older lads went in Sportsman and younger in Lewisham. I was in the Lewisham with the younger lot who were really ready to go. As kick off neared, about 2.30pm, people started filing out of the pubs to ground which is about a 10 to 15 minute walk away. About 10 or so lads peeled off, Cola, Big Jon, Tony F, Nicky, Peachy, Micky, Clem and a few others.

Cola: Here were the main and original members of the Section 5 crew. It was just the way it happened but it couldn't have worked out better. Most of the best rows are unplanned and spontaneous and what happened next was like a gift from the gods. We'd all split and gone different ways in the day but it just fell into place with us then walking to ground.

We got near the M5 motorway island and looked down and there were two coaches stuck at the traffic lights coming up the slip road. They were full of lads, we assumed to be Soul Crew with flags draped up windows. They were all chanting in the windows and about 20 or 30 of them jumped off the coach. There was no Old Bill and we just went into them straight away. Two lads got on the bus and as they got on they were getting booted as they tried to wade into them. It was a freezing cold day and one of the lads in a hat got a tremendous blow to the head by a copper as by then, the Old Bill were appearing as lads were scrapping outside the coach as well. Once they arrived you knew they would start filming and more of our lot arrived and got stuck in.

Chinda: Jon called me just as about 100 to 150 of us were walking up to it all. We piled in and were fighting on the slip road and back down onto the motorway and charging at the coaches in traffic. It was a right battle for ages, uproar. We backed them onto the motorway but we had the numbers to be fair and there were some normal fans on the coaches so we didn't attack them. We knew the cops were coming as well as more lads, we were the second wave I guess, so we carried onto the ground.

When the cops appeared they escorted the Cardiff off the coaches to the ground and they got attacked again en route by the younger lot and some Yew Tree lads. We knew if we hung around we'd get done for supposedly kicking it off so we'd left by then. It was rowdy in the ground and afterwards the cops were on top so nothing happened. We think there were a few without tickets but the police just put them in the ground anyway.

In the aftermath, about 15 or 20 of our lot were arrested and the cops tried to treat is as violent disorder and suggest it was pre-arranged. But we discovered the coaches were apparently meant to come off the motorway earlier than they did, at Frankly Services, but these didn't. In the end, lads were fined and banned. It was a good battle though. I spotted a big girl in amongst Cardiff who wanted the row. She seemed like a proper lad.

Chapter Sixteen

The Uplands to C-Wing HMP Winson Green – End of an Era

Jon: In August 2004 we were playing Villa at the Hawthorns and we met early doors in the Hargate Arms out of the way at the back of West Brom town centre. The early part of this day was uneventful really. Our numbers were big but it was pointless. The usual bullshit Villa phone call nonsense was in full flow with promises of them turning up. We had placed ourselves purposely on this side of town because it gave Villa easy opportunity to come from their side of town through Great Barr straight towards us. True to form, the bullshit calls continued and there was a Villa no-show, no shock there. It was clear they had no intention of showing so, the majority of our lads filtered towards the town centre. Phil, myself and a few others made our way up to the Sportsman where again a large number of our lot were out. A lot of this group were not at the Hargate Arms so we had a good firm, numbers and face-wise. Pre-game was uneventful so we went to the match which ended 1-1. But during, word went around that afterwards we were to make our way up towards the Royal Oak pub which was the direction Villa would head on their way back to their areas. Albion and Villa are only three or four miles apart so our areas overlap. The Royal Oak was full to bursting after the game. I would say roughly 200 present with a good contingent of our younger lads in evidence as well as some good older ones. This firm was more than good enough for Villa but the Old Bill had other ideas. They surrounded the pub so we were going no where. Villa were gathering at the Uplands pub which was a five minute walk from the Royal Oak. The police presence was frustrating because with what we had would have been a cracking scrap. Never mind, 1-0 to the Old Bill.

It became clear that nothing was going to happen so we started leaving the Oak, heading back up towards West Brom town centre. The Sportsman and the Lewisham are two big boozers and they were both packed full of lads and for the next two hours the bullshit phone calls were in meltdown. Villa were coming to us apparently, yet another load of empty threats and promises that never came to anything. They had no intention whatsoever of coming to us and if they did, it would have been a slaughter. Our numbers were enormous with a who's who of Albion faces from all through the years.The Old Bill were all over the High Street for a good amount of time so we held tight and didn't go anywhere for the time being. Carl C, Chinda and myself managed to sneak out of the backyard of the Sportsman and jump into Carl's car to go down to the Uplands to have a look at who was about, numbers and what the Old Bill were doing. We got down there and Chinda called a local Indian lad over who was outside the pub to ask him who and how many were inside. The lad said he knew they were Villa but didn't know any names and estimated there were 70-80 inside. We left and went back to the Sportsman. It was decided that after the police had left the area we'd get down to the Uplands as quickly as we could with as many as we could. I think the police leaving the area was wishful thinking on our part because they stayed put. After a while, Phil, Eamon, Carl and some others were getting impatient and finally 15 to 20 of us sneaked out of the back of the pub again en route to the Uplands. With these numbers we were going to be heavily outnumbered but this didn't matter one iota to Eamon and Carl and Uplands-bound we were.

I collected my car from nearby and made my way up West Brom High Street and back towards the ground. After rounding the motorway island Phil, Connor, Joseph and Keith came into view and I stopped and picked them up. We drove up the main Birmingham Road and turned off into Island Road, now within a short distance of the Uplands. I pulled through the dual carriageway cut through and dropped our lot off. There was no where to park and I wanted to get my car out of the area if a row was imminent, firstly to avoid getting it damaged and secondly, I didn't want to be nicked getting back into it. I drove round for a few minutes but simply could not park.

I went back down to where I had dropped off the lads and looked right towards the Uplands. I soon saw they hadn't waited for the others on their way and had gone down and confronted Villa outside the pub. I screamed onto the dual carriageway and shot down towards the action. The road was backed up with cars and when I got closer, my heart sank as there were three Old Bill filming everything with a hand held camera. I have got to be honest here because I was in two minds what to do - stay or go. To stay would mean a definite nicking. I looked down at the chaos and my mind was made up, I just couldn't leave my pals to it. Some did leave the scene without getting involved and I wouldn't knock them, it's their choice. I shot through the cut off, bumped my car up a pavement, jumped out and ran down to the action. My plans for getting my car out of the way were well and truly out of the window.

As soon as I arrived on the scene, I was hit with half a house brick straight in the bollocks. This took the wind out of me and it was fucking painful but I managed to pull myself together and the scene was this - 70 Villa and 20-ish Albion, as a few more had arrived separate to us. We were coming under heavy fire from missiles, bricks, bottles, glasses, bins, everything that wasn't nailed down. We returned everything with interest and were holding our own, standing our ground against far superior numbers but, numbers do not mean a thing. If you have got 20 lads who will stand-on against these numbers then the job is half done. I received a couple of digs and gave out one beauty which put the receiver straight on his arse. I then got involved in a bit of a one-on-one affair which involved punches being thrown from both sides. I didn't do too badly in this exchange and then my opponent was hit by a missile which took him out. The row was going backwards and forwards and still we were holding our own. Carl was doing some serious damage with an iron bar, it was like Big Ben chimes if you catch my drift. Eamon was as game as ever and Clem received a bang to the head which resulted in him taking the weapon off the Villa lad and filling him in with it. Phil was getting stuck in and I distinctly remember him relieving an opponent of his Stone Island cardigan and joyfully swinging it around his head beckoning the owner to come and collect it. Amongst all the chaos, that was a piss- take and amusingly enough the owner did make an attempt to retrieve it but was clattered before he managed to do so. Chinda and Khulla were at the forefront of everything that was going on and again another amusing sight was Chinda removing a lad's Lacoste T-shirt and giving him a few digs for his troubles. This was taking the piss big style. Carl continued to do serious damage with his bar which by now was bent like a banana and most of the other lads including Keith, Bail', Kendo, Connor, Symo and a few of the younger lot were playing their part. Obviously everyone was aware the Old Bill were filming. It was pointless to stop because in real terms, we were already nicked.

After a while Villa realised that we weren't budging and started pointing out that we were being filmed. But we pointed out that this was the case from word go so why worry now? They were flapping and running out of ideas. All we could do was to carry on as we were, standing our ground and picking people off. The fighting started more or less 100 yards away from the pub and shortly before the trouble stopped, we on the car park and we were the ones pushing forward. This tells a story in my eyes. We had done well and stood our ground. We had been pushed back at times and I don't find that hard to admit because that is the way it was but, we had done our fair share of pushing forward and in my estimation had thrown the most punches. Carl had done some serious damage with his bar. The sirens could soon be heard and it was apparent they were coming from the same direction as we had. Looking back up the road, all I could see was police vans coming down the wrong side of the dual carriageway. I decided it was time to go. I grabbed Phil and quickly we made our way to my car. Most of our lot had arrived in cars and they did the same thing. We all shot off and managed to escape and made our way back to the Sportsman. There were roughly 10 or 12 of us in cars and the other lot on-foot had been collared by the Old Bill and nicked.

In the Sportsman, we all relayed what had gone on and decided as a group we had done well but the general feeling was front doors were going to be banged off in the not too distant future. Not something to look forward to. As predicted, in October the first batch of dawn raids were carried out on our lot - Phil, Keith, Chinda and Connor were amongst them. This confirmed our fears and it was just a case of waiting for my turn and 6am on December 16 my front door was receiving a serious pounding. I hadn't long been in from work and it was obvious who it was so my partner, Karen, let them in. They explained why they were here and gave me a list of clothing that they wanted me to get for them. Shortly after I was handcuffed and taken away in an unmarked car with a police van following us on the way to Wednesbury police station to be questioned and charged. I kept schtum during questioning and just went no comment all the way. I have found this the best way over the years and when reaching court I usually blame the duty solicitor for my non co-operation. Over the next few months more of our lot were nicked and eventually when we were all done we numbered 22.

We were all bailed to appear at the police station on numerous occasions and then we were in Birmingham Magistrates' Court all charged with violent disorder. The case was referred to the crown court as it deemed to be too serious to be dealt with by magistrates. But it felt that the verdicts were already in before it even started as it was not looking good. We all knew we were up shit creek without a paddle but usually you, along with your brief, can try to sort out a lesser charge for an early guilty plea. But, they were having none of it. The arse was starting to twitch. I was given a copy of the video early doors and I scanned it for hours even in slow motion.

It cheered me up a bit because even though I was clearly evident in the film and on the stills photos the Old Bill had, I was seen to be doing very little in either. My optimism was severely blown away after being called into see my barrister at his office. He had done an edited version of the footage to show my involvement and you could clearly see that I was fighting and also the punch I'd thrown which led to the Villa lad being floored was captured in part. They also had footage of me brandishing a plank of wood that I'd picked up during the row. In my barrister's estimation I was fucked. He pointed out that being present alone was enough to be found guilty. I found this hard to believe but he obviously knew his stuff and I was not going to argue.

I was advised to plead guilty at the earliest opportunity to get the maximum credit from the judge. This was hard to swallow because I now knew I was going to prison. Phil, Clem, Amber and I were due for sentencing on the 1 August. The judge seemed like a crack-pot. In previous court appearances he was like a school headmaster talking down to five-year-old kids. We had no say in anything and the judge said we had no defence for our actions. The footage was played to a packed court room and afterwards we were individually pulled apart by the judge. When it came to sentencing, Clem and Phil got 20 months in prison and seven-year bans from football involving Albion and England, at home and abroad. I was next, getting 18 months and a seven-year ban. Amber on the other hand, had been charged with conspiracy to cause violent disorder, ie; he had been blamed for the whole affair. He had been well and truly stitched up because he had nothing whatsoever to do with the incident. The Old Bill had video footage of him leaving the Royal Oak earlier in the day in conversation on the phone with an anonymous Villa lad, who had called him out of the blue. As I said, well stitched up. He received three years and one month and a 10-year ban from football. This pissed me off as much as my own sentence. Admittedly Amber had been an active lad on the Albion scene for a good few years and been involved in court cases in recent times from which he had rather lucky escapes. Maybe the Old Bill were after him for past events or, more likely, they wanted a scape-goat for the organisation of this fairly major incident because really they had nothing that proved this was a pre-arranged fight - the basis for their violent disorder charge.

After the event, a so-called top boy from Villa referred to Albion in a book as the most tooled-up firm they had ever come up against. Fuck me son, you need to get out more often. One lad with an iron bar? He, amongst others, also stated at the end we had run. Total rubbish. We only left the scene when the police arrived en masse. If they had not arrived, we'd still be there now. Bearing in mind the numbers difference we consider that we did rather well. Nothing more, nothing less and along the way we took the piss in certain instances. Simple as that.

I will not go like-for-like and slag our rivals off. Villa and Wolves have got good lads, I have no problem whatsoever in saying that and with the reputation Birmingham have it is pointless in me talking about them. Their reputation speaks for itself. Villa's C Crew/Steamers and Wolves Subway were quality, well organised firms. My point on all this is, that over the last 15-20 years we have more than held our own against all of the above mentioned and Birmingham are the only one out of the three that have fronted us in our town. Villa and Wolves have failed miserably against us for the vast majority of those years. Villa's idea of football violence is sitting in close proximity to their ground surrounded by the police. On the rare occasions they do actually travel anywhere, more often than not they are followed by a police film crew or the police are fully aware of their exact movements and intentions.

Phil, Clem, Amber, Keith, Eamon, Carl and myself were all on C Wing in HMP Birmingham - aka Winson Green. Most of us worked together and I must say, in difficult circumstances these lads were a pleasure to be around. We kept each other going and had a bit of a laugh along the way. Chinda, Simo and Kulla were also in Winson Green but they were on another wing so we didn't see much of them. Amber was my pad mate and I cannot speak highly enough of him. He had been done up like a kipper but he showed what a strong character he is. He got on with it and he kept me highly amused for the five months I was padded up with him. He's a genuine bloke who sums up Black Country folk, salt of the earth. He and his pals from in and around the Tiger pub on the Yew Tree estate are amongst Albion's best lads. But really, they all get my maximum respect. They showed strength in adversity both at the Uplands and prison.

We were also on the same wing and work area as some of the Villa contingent and these lads as a whole were sound. But I did meet the notorious Fowler for the first time. Based on reputation and hearsay alone I'd heard he was a complete fool. I had seen/faced him a few times during incidents but here was a chance to get to know him and make my own judgements. At first, he confirmed my suspicions as I heard nothing but nonsense but after a while and a few decent conversations, I thought he was okay and in general, a decent bloke. Leading up to his court appearance, he insisted to a few of us that he had done nothing apart from just being there. I thought fair enough, at least he was being honest and, despite obvious rivalries, I hoped he would have a decent result in court which he did. But on his return to prison after court, he returned to his usual nonsense self over the following days and weeks which was disappointing. Phil, who was working alongside me in the kitchens, witnessed Fowler's new account of his involvement at the Uplands which was now the total opposite to his earlier version of no involvement at all. Apparently, he went windmilling through our firm, knocking half of them out and put Eamon on his arse.

Over the following days, me, Phil and Carl C – Eamon's cell mate – discussed his new, warped version of events. Carl was gobsmacked and without hesitation told Eamon. The next evening, Eamon confronted Fowler in full view of the whole wing.

It led to Eamon giving Fowler a smack which resulted in a straightner in the recess. A well-known but neutral lad from Handsworth, who was in the shower at the time of the straightner, told us what happened. It lasted no time at all due to the screws being on the scene very quickly and was broken up but, the stories that came out of Winson Green following that little scuffle, sum Villa and Fowler up to a tee. Apparently our two lads Eamon and Carl were put out of action for weeks. Fucking hilarious! That's the biggest load of bollocks I've ever heard and we have heard plenty from Villa. Eamon is no slouch and Carl C would murder 99.9% of anything that Villa could put up. After this and my release from prison, my name was put in the frame for opening my mouth and causing this argument and subsequent incident. I was part of the afore-mentioned conversation, no problem on that score but at the end of the day the blame lay firmly at Fowler's feet. He was everything I had been told and more and if he is the best Villa can muster post C Crew/Steamers then is it any wonder they are so poor? The summary of him in the Zulu book is 100% nailed-on.

This book to me is a blessing in disguise it has given me the opportunity to get things off my chest and put things across from our perspective. I would like to take this opportunity to thank Karen, 'my rock', for being the lady she is. She showed amazing strength through everything and stood by me. For that I'll always love her and never forget what she has done for me as well the rest of my family who also stood by me and supported me 100% as did my friends. The visits and letters were never-ending and that means a lot when you are banged up for 16 hours a day, believe me. When my ban is up I'll be going to games with my kids. It's over for me now. Lesson learned but my blood is navy blue and white and always will be.

Chapter Seventeen
The Black Country Derby

Tony: A lot has been said in books and the like about the Black Country derby and the firms involved and unfortunately you've only had it from a Wolves perspective. To say it's been one-eyed from their spokesman, Gilly or, Bullshitter Gilly, as Wally says in Zulus, is one massive understatement. Yes, we all know the Subway were a decent firm, blah blah blah, but they went ages ago. But to Gilly and his Yam Yam Army, well, read on and make your own mind up because every single word I'm about to write is the truth.

Every firm has been turned over by their rivals one time or another right? Well, not according to him. So let's begin putting his wrongs right with a few of us telling our side of the story about incidents over the years.

Chinda: It was a boiling hot day when we played Wolves at theirs on a Sunday, the second game of the 1995/6 season. In previous years we've always gone to theirs on the train and the Old Bill always used to get us. You just know that's going to happen.

This time, someone said let's get everyone together and meet at the Wheatsheaf pub on the High Street in West Brom. It was one of our main lad's pubs so you knew all the faces would be there. It was kept quiet so the right people were there while others went to meet at Dudley Port. There was a 100-plus in the Wheatsheaf and one of the lads knew a bus driver and what route he'd be on so we were waiting for him to take us. He appeared with a double-decker with "Not in Service" on the front and we all squashed on and those who couldn't fit on went in minibuses. We went straight to Wolverhampton and got into Bilston Street just after 2pm where we got off. We expected to see the Old Bill but they weren't there so we turned a corner and saw a pub, also called the Wheatsheaf. It was a really, really hot day and there were about 40 of them drinking outside in the sun and we went straight into them. People were actually getting lifted up and put through windows. One lad was knocking people out for fun. We just went straight through them. There was another pub about 40 yards further on, Shamus O Brian's I think, and there were more there so we attacked it. A few of them went for us but we just ran them up the road. They could see how many there was of us.

We carried on walking up past lots more pubs, there was a stretch of them for about 300 or 400 yards, and all they did was lock them up and stay inside. We went to the Varsity pub where they had all gathered and they all went inside and held the doors and wouldn't come out. The windows were put through and they still wouldn't come out. We were in the town for about 15 minutes and not one of them came near us. They outnumbered us but never capitalised on it. The coppers came as the windows went through on the Varsity pub. They'd been waiting for us at the train station so we'd surprised them too. But as the police rounded us up, the lads all decided to come out of the pub and started giving it the large one but, the damage is done by then boys. No one was arrested either, nothing.

We knew they would all be pissed off by what we'd done so after the game we came out the ground and a few of their older lads did try to come at us, coming out the bushes to have a go. The Old Bill was all around us and there were a few skirmishes as we walked. About 25-30 of us got away from the Old Bill and we moved away and got in with a load of Wolves who thought we were with them too. We marched down with them and as we got down about 30 yards there was no police with us so we went straight into them. We were only about 100 yards from a pub called the Elephant and Castle and we went to attack that when they went running into it. But, I stopped as I knew the girl's dad who owned it so I just left it. We caught a bus from the outskirts of Wolverhampton and we then had phone calls to say meet in Coseley. The Old Bill tried to stop us but there wasn't much they could do. When we got there, there were about 20 of them and about 60 of us and we chased them - outnumbered them again -and that was about it for that day. It was pure piss-take that day in the way we dominated in their city. In 1997, they did have it better and there was more of a stand off

(as KJ, one of the lads who was there, explains below). But, after 1995 a lot
of lads didn't turn out because they thought, you go to Wolves and
nothing happens, you wait around and they don't show. We did them
two times in 1995 and in 1998 but at least we made the effort to get into
their area, something they never done to us.

* * * * * * *

KJ: We were playing at Wolves on a Sunday, I think it was 1997, and
it was a midday kick off. A lot of our lads were banned at the time so
we didn't take much of a firm but still had a few decent lads and main
faces going over, about 60-odd. We decided to get the number 79 bus
from West Bromwich into Wolverhampton city centre. Unbeknown to
us, they had sent some spotters over to West Brom, where we were
meeting, to see how we were travelling and what numbers we would
be bringing. We boarded the bus which was mainly full of shirts. When
it pulled into Wolverhampton we decided to get off one stop before the
city centre to avoid the Old Bill and hopefully bump into Wolves. The
spotters followed the bus, something we were still unaware of, and
were on their phones to tell others where we got off. As we turned
a corner, we saw what must have easily been 50 to 100 Wolves lads
running up the street towards us and the shout went up "They're here!
They're here!" At the front of our lot was Clem, Phil, Big Keith, me and
Lynx and with no Old Bill about, we took our positions in the road.

Wolves were about 100 yards away from us throwing pint pots,
bottles and bricks, whatever they could. As we lined up, we realised
our numbers were getting smaller and smaller and when Wolves were
within 20 yards of us, we realised that Albion had run off and left
us five. At that point, we started to back off as while we were game
lads, we were heavily outnumbered. YES! The ultimate shame. We ran
from Wolves. As we backed off around the corner, we realised they
had caught Lynx. Phil and Keith went back to help him realising more
Wolves lads were on us. I remember Clem shouting "West Brom stand!"
At that point, there were only about 10 of us who stood in the road
and were expecting Wolves come at us as we were easily outnumbered
but, they started dancing in the road and shouting abuse at us. Now
we heard the sirens but a copper on a motorbike must have been one
of first to arrive and he got off his bike and CS gassed Clem and me
point-blank in the face. Then more Old Bill turned up and escorted

us to the ground. I wanted to write this true and detailed view just to prove we are not one of those firms who go everywhere and never get done. It hurts me to say it but yes, we did get done by Wolves.

* * * * * * *

Tony: On this particular Saturday morning in 1998, we all met in the Wheatsheaf pub in West Brom and what a fuckin' firm we had. Not so much the quantity but the quality. All the main heads were there and we knew the Old Bill would be expecting us to go on the train, which a lot did but not all the main lads. Everyone was pumped up and mad for it to go off. We just knew we'd never get a better chance to get into their city centre than today but, I for one had my doubts. Firstly, could we all get on one bus? Secondly would the police get to us first? It was 50-50 but we were gonna' give it a shot. I just knew we could put things right if we could get amongst 'em. By 1.30-ish the signal came that the bus had arrived and all 96 of us - yes, I counted every last one - came out the boozer. We couldn't believe our luck, our top boy knew the fucking driver, who in turn let us all on. To be honest, if the Old Bill had pulled this bus over they would have had a field day. It must have been in every breach of public safety rule going. There was so much weight up stairs the floor was buckling and the ceiling had come away. Anyway, we got off at the New Inns, just outside the city centre. One of our lads, Kendo, was pretty local so knew the best way to get in undetected through the shitty backstreets. It seemed to take ages and everyone kept saying "We're gonna' get sussed". But, all of a sudden we were faced with a main duel carriageway, with a row of bushes through the middle and we knew if we could make it over, we were almost there. In twos, threes, and fours we ran over first to the bushes, then across onto a car park. How we all managed it, I still don't know. Now, we only had the car park to negotiate and then up to the top of the road where we knew two of their main pubs were. We were almost jogging up the road to our targets, turn right and "We're fucking here. Come on". Then there they were, right in front of us.

The roar was ear-piercing as we were met with a hail of glasses and bottles. Some of our lot had collected some ammo' on the trek and returned fire. The two firms got to grips with one another with little scraps going on all over the road. The sound of glass smashing and the smell of CS gas filled the air. I noticed we were well on top by now and we charged Wolves again and all, except the odd one who couldn't get away, legged it all over the place. We'd fuckin done them proper. They wouldn't be able to deny this one surely? Like I said, they'd probably forgotten. The now very irate police came from behind and in front of us and blocked us off down a side street, by the Express and Star building. We were going crazy to get back at them again but the Old Bill led us towards the ground. They had real trouble keeping us apart on the way but just as we arrived at the back of the John Ireland Stand, we broke the escort. Wolves were by our turnstiles whacking a few normal fans and we landed on them big style. This time they ran straight away before the Old Bill got us in the ground. After the game, there was a free-for-all right outside the exits. It was pitch black and anyone was punching anyone but it was quickly broken up and we were all marched to the train station. Wolves did try to get at our escort but the Old Bill kept chasing them off. But to top a fantastic day off we won the game 1-0. Ha Ha. As you can see, all-in-all, apart from the odd head being stitched up from the throwing at the start, we pissed all over them. I don't know why that wasn't in Gilly's book?

The truth is, I could waste the whole book on their exaggerations and lies but I'll put as much right as I can in one chapter. There's the time they smashed up the Halfway House before a game one year, which is supposedly one of "our" pubs. I've never been in there, nor have 90% of our firm. It's about a mile from the town centre, in a desolate bit nobody goes to. About 10 of our lads - two car loads - went down there to see if Wolves were coming to our town for once, as we thought it was the route we thought they'd take. To be fair, about 100 did turn up and on seeing these few lads outside the pub, instead of arranging something obviously saw it as an easy kill. So the brave Wolves lads steamed our scouts who ran through the pub and escaped out the back over the wall, to their car. The Dog-heads then smashed fuck out of an almost empty pub - except for a few old Asians playing cards - before the Old Bill rounded them up and marched them to the ground. They've bragged about that for years but why? Wally was right again eh? I will give Gilly the one about smoke-bombing Oddfellows, although Wolves ran and kept running for miles afterwards. Some of theirs were knocking on peoples' doors begging to be let in and the ones that were caught got a bit of a beating - one lad had his ear bitten off and another had a big plant pot dropped on his head. There was concern that he was dead at first. But there weren't 200 coming out after them, like they claim, more like 40 tops. Fuck me, we're talking three or four hours after the game ended on a Sunday night and, remember Wolves ran for their lives.

They did run about 60 of our mainly younger lads in 1997 but, apart from that, I can't remember a time when I've been present that we've backed off from them. I remember one Sunday around 1999 when we broke away from the escort and doubled back through the coach car park. There were about 60 of us. When they spotted us, it was like 200 Linford Christies running towards us full-pelt. We didn't budge and they put the brakes on, just in time for the police to get between us. I can still remember Jay asking this half-caste Dog-head if they wanted to borrow an A-Z to find their way to West Brom. After the main event in 1998 that I mentioned earlier, they made a big fuss that they were coming for us proper, so we took it seriously. We all met up early in the Prince Albert, just off the Lyng Estate in West Brom and let Wolves know where we would be waiting. As the clock ticked by they kept ringing telling us they'd be landing soon. Then about 20 to 30 minutes before kick-off they rang to say they had indeed landed. They'd landed alright, four fucking miles away down the Soho Road in Handsworth. Honestly, how the fuck could we get to them in that time with the Old Bill everywhere by then? Oh, they loved it. They marched to the Hawthorns, smashing windows at pubs full of shirters then rang us saying they'd done us and they've even got some Plymouth lads with them to prove it. We were still a fucking mile away from the ground by then.

I swear, no matter what strokes we have pulled on them they never admit it. Don't get me wrong, I have worked with the odd one who has admitted many of the things I've written about but, unfortunately it's the ones who put the stories into print that get the airplay. We even had the cheek to try the bus trick the very next time we played them and this time the Old Bill got us just past the car park but Wolves were no where to be seen. The year after that, about 150 of us went on the Metro tram. We told them hours before, even offering a meet in Bilston en route. They declined and told us they'd meet us off the tram instead but as we pulled in the only people to meet us was the police. However, away from the cameras and out of print, they have actually admitted to not turning up, firmed-up at the Albion. Every time some of their lads put it down to a lack of tickets. But on the other hand, we always turn up proper, home and away, as it's so easy to get tickets for Molineux due to our scarfers being too frightened to go in fear of attacks. They have a reputation throughout the country, wrongly or rightly, of attacking your every-day, normal football fan.

Like most firms, they have good lads amongst them and over the years, have probably done more away than us. However, I really do think we have proved more than a match for them at the Black Country Derby. But, remember Gilly's side of everything and remember it's by a so-called Wolves top-boy who on film, when fronted by an Albion lad outside the Hawthorns, claimed he was "Albion mate". Enough said I think.

* * * * * * *

Cola: After a midweek game at ours in the late-Nineties, the West Brom coppers said they didn't want to police a night match again after what went on. We wanted to meet Wolves in Smethwick, away from the Old Bill but they ended up in escort and that plan just didn't happen. We met at the Rising Sun pub in West Bromwich town centre and went on to the Cricketers before about 100-150 of us walked along the Metro tram line towards the ground as we wanted to ambush them as they came down Halfords Lane. We walked in silence pretty much, as some stayed in touch with them to find out where they were. There was a police helicopter above but it never saw us. When we got near to Halfords Lane we stopped and waited, all quiet so we could surprise them. We had to be careful and not appear too soon so people carried on finding out where they were on the road. I think there were about four black Mariahs, motorcycles and police around them but the cops did not know what was going on with us. Also, I think the game had kicked off so there weren't too many fans around, just stragglers really. We waited and waited and they would say what street they were going past as they got nearer. My heart was starting to race and some were pissing about doing the odd press-up and stretches for a laugh just to pass the time really. It had worked out well so far but we had to time it right. They said there were three vehicles in front of their escort and we were ready to pounce.

Now, whether a couple of our lads were flapping or they wanted to be heroes, I don't know but, they spoilt a very delicate operation as they ran out, way too soon and half way into the police at the front. We needed the coppers to pass so we could get to Wolves but they were right there instead and tried to block us off. But, we all charged into them and opened them up and got stuck in. The coppers went on the back heel at first, and then re-grouped but that gave us more of a chance to get in and past them. There must have been about 50 to 60 tops of Wolves lads and we got into them and that was it, running battles all along Halfords Lane. A couple of lads got bit by dogs and they managed to separate us and tried to get Wolves into the ground. At this time, the Albion were making a lot of noise, in my opinion, turning up with numbers every week, same faces and all that. It was organised and wasn't like little groups in the past and the cops knew this. We re-grouped and the police tried to charge us two or three times to get us back, this was right by Halfords Lane, the main doors to ground, and we just wouldn't move. Not one bit. They'd charge, we'd exchange blows with them, they'd back off, we'd re-group and they'd come again. It was like a military operation or something. It didn't seem like they were keen on nicking people. There must have been about four lines of coppers and they'd shout "Get back!", but we would not move. Our line just would not break. I remember one lad, who isn't even a hoolie just a local rower. He thought he'd have a go with cops and was stood there beckoning at them, single-handed. I was shouting him back but in one charge by the police he got caught up in it and found himself at the back of it, stuck on the other side. It was comical as they seemed to go round him - think he got nicked in the end but let off later. We didn't get in to the ground until towards the end of the first half - it lasted a long time that one did. There were a few minor incidents afterwards but the cops were on top by then.

* * * * * * *

Big Jon: In my opinion, the build up to an incident at the Fox and Dogs pub in West Brom shows how Gilly cannot be trusted. In fact, it shows how treacherous he is. One of our lads, Sharky, was in regular contact with Gilly on a sort of friendly basis. I was also in contact with him but mainly in the build up to games between our clubs. During a conversation between Sharky and Gilly, our man was asked where he drank after the games at our place. Sharky probably thought this was an innocent question but it was not and he said he usually drank in the Vine, which isn't really a lad's pub more of a family venue serving food. On the day of this particular incident, Wolves were playing at Walsall and we were at home to Swindon. No disrespect to Swindon but interest in this game was virtually nil. We didn't have many about and it was a quiet day on the whole. Rumours of Wolves showing up in

West Brom after their game had been discussed but they wasn't taken seriously because we'd heard similar things so many times before. After our game, the few of us that were about had gradually filtered down to the town centre. It was quiet with not many people about at all, there were about 10-15 of us and we were drinking in the Billiard Hall. At roughly 7.30pm I got a call from one of our older lads, Steve B from Whiteheath. He said Wolves had been into the Vine, had a good look around and then left heading towards the town centre. He added that he and his pal would follow them and he'd keep me informed. I put our lot in the picture and without much more hesitation we were on the move.

We walked quickly through the main shopping area towards the top part of the High Street and Steve called me again to let me know Wolves had gone into the Fox and Dogs pub and stayed put. On our way up towards the High Street, loads of calls were made to numerous lads who lived nearby. They were all on their way. The pub is only a few hundred yards on to the top part of the High Street. As we approached it, the 15 to 20 of us were spotted. Wolves came piling out, numbering in the region of 40. A whole host of missiles were launched at us including bottles, bricks and glasses. We just stepped back and let the missiles completely miss their targets then we charged forward. Wolves simply scattered everywhere and hastily retreated to the safety of the pub. The next part shocked me to a certain extent. When most of the Wolves had gone back inside, they actually shut plenty of their own lads out and left them at the mercy of us. Obviously, we took full advantage and seriously clattered them while another four or five of our lot showed up on the scene, including Joseph, C, Sweat and several of his pals. Joseph quickly sprang into action and gave one of the Wolves lot a good pasting against the shutters of a neighbouring shop. I was right in the doorway of the pub giving another Wolves lad a good hiding with an old milk crate. I must have hit him 10 or 12 times around the face and head with it. I then pushed him into the door and his so-called friends actually shoved him back out. I then gave this lad one final dig and he was finished and on the floor.

Clem, Chinda, Alan, Steve Guy, Jolly, Quint and the rest of our lot were getting stuck in. All the Wolves lot shut out of the pub, were now out of the game and done over. One amusing part preceding these initial exchanges was Carlton, the very large half-caste Wolves face, wobbling onto a bus and disappearing into the distance leaving his friends to it. Fucking hilarious. At this point, two Old Bill turned up in a car and Wolves took this as an opportunity to come out and try to save face. Gilly appeared for the first time and until that moment we did not think he was present. He was brandishing a stool and fronting it up. The Old Bill were calling for assistance and Sweat came from the side of Gilly and gave him a little rattler on the jaw. My opportunity now appeared so I shot forward and landed three or four meaty digs into him which forced him back against the wall. Several more of our lot now surrounded Gilly and gave him a good pasting. His so-called friends including Operation Growth- grass Howey, Tyson and several others simply stood in the shadows watching it all unfold. The rest of the Wolves rabble continued to cower in the safety of the pub.

During the chaos, another amusing thing happened. The landlord and lady were in the upstairs window of the pub throwing out bottles at our lot. They were totally unaware that Wolves had occupied their pub and we were West Brom lads on the scene sorting them out. All they could see was their pub being smashed to bits. The front of the pub was a sorry state as was Gilly. Several Wolves lads had received a serious beating in the initial clashes and the rest had simply hidden and stayed in the pub. One of our lads was hit on the head with a bottle thrown from upstairs and had a nasty cut which required stitches. I, as per normal during these incidents, had been hit by a missile. What it was I do not know but, my ear was black, blue and purple for weeks afterwards.

To clarify what I said about Gilly being treacherous and not to be trusted, Sharky was on decent terms with him, not good friends but it was a respectful, honest kind of thing. Lads across the country deal with or are in contact with lads in other firms, through international games and travels amongst other things. I suggest that these lads, as a whole, would not do the dirty on each other where possible. By going straight to the Vine, in my opinion that shows Gilly as the person he is. I had told Sharky many times not to trust him. My advice was spot on and Gilly has shown many times since this incident what a treacherous kind of person he really is. He has been done by Albion lads over more times than I care to remember and he has deserved it and instigated it on every occasion. After this incident, I spoke to Gilly on the phone. All he was worried about was what our lot had to say on this Fox and Dogs incident. I said we thought he was a complete clown before this episode and basically nothing had changed. His version of events was rather amusing so was his estimation of numbers involved. He was in hospital with concussion after his hiding and I suggest his bang on the head had severely affected his memory and ability to be honest. Another part of Gilly's excuse was that a large percentage of the Wolves lads present were "divs" from areas like Kidderminster. Slagging his own lads off? Unforgivable and his own mates had stood by watching him being filled in. What did he think of them? On our approach to the pub I didn't know what to expect and with our numbers I thought we had a job on our hands but my fears were unfounded. Wolves were severely embarrassed. Fair-play and respect to our lot. A job well done with again less numbers.

The last game of the 2000/01 season we were playing at Preston North End. This fixture created a lot of interest firstly because we were pushing for promotion, secondly because of the Blackpool weekend piss up factor. Loads of lads were due to travel north and I along with many of my mates decided to make a long weekend of it and travel up on the Friday. About 15 to 20 of us, mainly Bearwood lads like Alfie, Jonah and Kev, arrived in Blackpool late in the afternoon. We dropped our stuff in our hotels and hit the pubs and we soon discovered that quite a few more of our lads had had the same idea in making it a long weekend and were out drinking. We were out along the front and stayed late on into the night, numbering about 70 with lads from Worcester and a fair few of the Brummie Albion lads from Quinton. Bristol City were playing up North the following day so we expected to bump into a few of their lads but this didn't materialise but a fight was not far away.

We were all in Yates's having a good night when Mike, one of our lads, came over saying some lads on the dance floor were giving it loads and messing him about. So three or four of us walked over and watched to see what the crack was and we saw that these lads were bullying and messing anyone near them about - male or female. I casually walked over and knocked one of them clean out. The others panicked and ran in all directions before the doormen appeared and started trying to wrestle me to the ground. But they failed because I'm a big lump and in the end they let me stay and threw the others out. That was about it trouble-wise for the rest of the night.

Leading up to this weekend, I had been in touch with Gilly from Wolves on numerous occasions. He said they were also travelling to Blackpool this weekend so if this true, it was going to be very interesting. Early the next morning my phone was ringing like crazy - our lot en route and Wolves asking how many we had. I must admit I didn't take Gilly seriously when he claimed they were also going to be in Blackpool, nor did the rest of our lads when I told them, but if the phone calls were correct, then fair-play. I thought if they've got the balls to show up here with all our lads due here then good luck to them - they'll need it. When it was evident they were indeed Blackpool-bound, I got on the phone to all our lot and told them what was developing. A few more phone calls later, I knew our lot were either all over Blackpool, still en route or more than likely still hanging out of the women they had pulled the night before. I called Jonah and arranged to meet him at the Dutton Arms as soon as possible. We got a drink and went outside and enjoyed the hot, sunny weather. We were stood talking for 10-15 minutes when there was a knock at the window of the pub and I turned around to see Gilly with a broad grin on his face. I acknowledged him and was surprised because I wasn't sure they'd show up. We carried on drinking but were obviously now on our guard. Although I was on, shall we say, decent terms with Gilly, this would not stop the other Wolves lads from filling us in if they felt like doing so. About 10 minutes later Jonah and I left to go and have a look about to see if any decent numbers of our lot were about. In the next pub, there was a fair-sized mob of our lot but they were more shirters than lads. We had a discussion and I said we should hold fire for the time being and wait for our main mob to show up. Jonah and I moved on again up towards the Manchester pub which contained a large number of our lads, about 120-odd. The word on the Wolves presence quickly spread and as we were about to move, we heard that the shirters from the last pub had jumped the gun and confronted them - exactly what we had said not to do. Apparently, 15 of our well known faces had turned up off the train and the shirters took this as a sign to attack, but it backfired.

Wolves were heavily armed with blades, gas and a whole host of other weapons. Most of the shirters backed off leaving a few brave souls and the 15 lads to get on with it. Our lads didn't fair too badly but obviously the shirters backing off and a few of our lot receiving digs was a major victory on Wolves part. Their lad Howey, was seen brandishing a blade, was taken out with a bottle. Our chance of landing on Wolves big-style was gone. Minutes after the row went off, a massive firm of our lot were in the area but it was a waste of time as the Old Bill were everywhere. They surrounded the pub and put all of their efforts into getting us away from the scene. Our lot, now in the hundreds, were everywhere. Toby was nicked for carrying CS gas and a telescopic truncheon after being in the thick of the action, no surprise there. Toby is a good, solid lad and obviously his involvement hadn't gone unnoticed. The Old Bill were after him and they got their man. Shortly after we were pushed away by mounted police and continuous baton charges, we dispersed into little groups and moved into all the little side streets. We went to a pub called the Bridge and in no time at all the pub was heaving with our lot, about 200 to 300. Our lads were on the phones to Wolves telling them to let it all calm down and we'd be down but, in reality I think there was no way the Old Bill were going to let anything more occur. Our numbers in the Bridge continued to grow and the phone calls between the two firms continued. JL called Gilly and once again told him/them to let it die down and we'd be down but it was pointless with the massive Old Bill presence. It was day-over already.

As the day wore on Cola and I went for a look about to see who we could find. After a short while, we found the coach Wolves had come up on parked in a coach park not far from where the trouble had kicked off. We got on and had a word with the driver, blagging him we were Wolves. We asked him what time and where we were being picked up from. He said up by the Tower at midnight. We headed back to the Bridge pub and told people what we had found out. We decided the best bet was to let it lie for the time being and meet up by the Tower at 11.45pm and catch them boarding their coach home. Everyone eventually went off in their own groups to different pubs. I wasn't in a good mood to be honest because I thought we had missed a big chance to deal with our old foes but, hopefully we could catch them later. At 11.45pm loads of our lads were out. We waited around for a good length of time but no coach showed up. We guessed the coach driver had sussed us earlier and got word to the Wolves lot and rearranged their departure point. Now it was definitely day-over and to top it all off the Old Bill arrived and gave us major hassle and Section 60s galore. In the aftermath, Wolves claimed that after the afternoon row, the vast majority of them had caught the train home. We knew different because they were seen in numerous pubs and clubs during the day/night.

Football violence books in general is usually one way with never been done, never been run nonsense but Wolves to their credit showed up in Blackpool. That, in my opinion is good enough and they get my respect for doing so. There's a saying in football violence circles that you can only do what is put in front of you and Wolves were on top in the incident, no question of that. Our pissed-up shirters well and truly fucked it up but fair-play to our 15 lads along with a few others who did have a go and stand their ground and fair-play and respect to Wolves for turning up. Ifs, buts and maybes are pointless now but, going by past incidents with Wolves and this particular group, if the firm on the way to the Dutton Arms had landed on them they would have been murdered and the same goes for the firm in the Bridge later in the day. I have no problem in writing this part because I feel honesty is the best way.

The following day in Preston we had loads out but the day was uneventful. The game was a nothing game because we had already qualified for the play-offs. Hundreds of our lot had fake tickets, most of these were stopped entering the ground. Back in Wolverhampton we heard they had a celebration party for "doing Albion". Funny. Good luck to them - if we had a party for every time we have done them over the last 15-20 years, we'd all be dead with liver failure.

And Finally

Snarka: Writing this book with Tony and Jon has brought back some great and some not so great memories. We have all tried to be as honest as possible and while we may not like other football teams, I suppose we all have a respect for other lads who have stood and fought for their teams over the years. We have tried not to belittle anyone as on their day, any firm can and beat anyone. Personally, it was never the violence it was the camaraderie, the sense of belonging the love of football, my mates, the clothes, the laughs, the atmosphere and, of course the Albion. But, saying that, I did enjoy a good punch-up.

It's very humbling to hear such good comments about me from most of Albion's firm, young and old, it's much appreciated. I got out of it at the right time for different reasons – a big mortgage and playing to a good level on Saturdays were just two of them. I now go with my wife and kids and even sponsor some of the players - I've even been known to eat a prawn sandwich. I still see some of the old faces and now they all have their kids with them. We had our time and we enjoy a good rattle about them.

To any young lad thinking of doing it now, I'd say think about it, times have changed. Is it worth it? That's up to you. Have I any regrets as Sid Vicious once sang? Too few to mention. I hope you have enjoyed reading the book as much as we enjoyed writing it. Special thanks must go to Caroline, without her help it would have stayed just a dream. Thanks Caroline.

Snarka - The Clubhouse

Big Jon: On the August 1 2004, I had a severe wake up call, an 18-month prison sentence in HMP Winson Green in Birmingham for trouble with Villa at the Uplands pub. The sentence made me realise how lucky I'd been during my most active period with the firm, from the mid-Nineties until 2004. It made me realise how I had total disregard for the law and the consequences. I'd been very lucky to only receive cautions and lucky escapes at football games. Numerous times in my stories, I've talked about other football violence books and that I prefer honesty but, some are not remotely in touch with reality or fact. Over the past 10 years, I've seen plenty television documentaries and read many books where many references are made to our firm.

One particular person who has talked about us was Gilly, the village idiot with Wolves. Obviously writing a book about Wolves he is going to mention West Brom and the rivalry that exists but his obsession with our lot has seen him receive numerous beatings and our lads receive numerous jail terms. It has gone beyond books. His involvement in documentaries and a book is laughable. All he has done over the years talk complete crap. I recently picked up a book written by Boatsy from Notts Forest, who I thought were decent in their day. I had a quick scan but quickly put it back after reading that they "took the piss" in our end one year. Yet another dreamer. Twenty were led out and escorted to the away end and they were very thankful I may add. I could go on and on in my references to things said by other individuals or firms but to be honest it's pointless but these are a couple of gripes I wanted to get off my chest. I'm sure lads in other firms have similar feelings and disagree about incidents they've read in books and maybe it will happen once you've read ours but we feel we've been honest.

I consider that our side has needed telling for many years and people that have simply written me or us off, do not know what they are talking about. Also, people on our own side who bitch about things, even as far as who is involved in this book, need to wise-up and realise we are doing this for everyone. There are better and more organised firms than us, not a problem on that score but I am 100% sure that we could give most firms in the country a run for their money. I can easily give our rivals respect. Villa and Wolves have more than their fair share of good lads and they deserve respect for their C Crew and Subway days respectively. What we have faced since as a whole we has not impressed us but, I'm not going to turn this into in to a personal vendetta, as the saying goes, actions speak louder than words.

With regards to firms I have faced over the years and all this top five nonsense, I don't really go in for that business. I will say that I rate Spurs very highly and I consider them the best in London and one of the best in the country. My thoughts on Blues are well documented in this book. I do have a personal interest because many of my friends are Blues as are some of my relatives. As for other firms like Cardiff, Pompey et al, I consider we have had a good pop at most of them. Man United are massive and we've also had a good go at them at ours in recent times.

Regarding those involved in the book, Snarka has told some good tales and is a genuine bloke and has got my respect 100%. Tony is also very well respected amongst our lads and I've seen him right at the forefront of many a battle over the years. He has done the intelligent thing for a good number of years now as at the end of the day the choice between your missus, kids and a good comfortable life or a prison cell is any easy one to make. His input is spot-on and in fact I have never known anyone with a better memory. He pipped me to one incident I wanted to cover, Wolves '98 but he's done a good job and that bus trick will long live in the memory - he did miss out our lot following the bus in taxis though. Peachy again needs no introduction and he along with Clem, Keron, Bail' and the rest of the Great Barr lads make up what is one of the best groups of lads amongst the firm, One person I cannot talk highly enough about is Chinda, a little pocket dynamo. He is genuine and very generous when we have been involved together doing recent fundraising events. Cola again, is also a genuine lad and was our voice in the Stone Cross/Yew Tree areas amongst others and he was a great help at all times.

Me and Joey have had a bit of, shall we say, turbulent friendship over the years. I think shit-stirring by certain unknown individuals soured what I thought was a decent friendship but in recent times we've had many chats and cleared the air. I never stopped respecting him but couldn't understand where certain kinds of nonsense were coming from and his name always seemed to be in the frame when I was the victim of certain gossip-mongers. Bowie is a hearsay kind of thing for me because what I know about him is what I have been told by others but, I was chuffed when I managed to get in touch with him through a Blues face I know. It's a major coup on our part that he is involved. Phil again is another good lad. He was the get-up-and-go part of the firm for many years, not one to hang about.

I conclude my input by paying respect to the lads not involved in the book but very much part of our firm: The Bearwood lads with Alfie my best pal being the figurehead, a rock for me and always there with help and support, Jonah is the same and brothers Ant and Alan, game as they come.

The Nuneaton lads, Tony, Jamie, Thommo, Pete, good lads and good friends. All the Oldbury lads, Phil E, Carl C, Dougie, Keith A, Connor, all good lads and all very good friends. RIP to Ronnie Bennett and Craig Fryer.

Thanks to Steve Clifton, who took the group photos and Dan of Countylads for the graphic design. Brothers Stevie and Daz G, again great lads and good friends and the Blackheath lads, mainly Big Dave, who is a great bloke good friend.

On a final note I must involve Caroline in my respect list so-to-speak as from day one she has been a massive help. We all cannot speak highly enough about her. She knows her stuff without doubt and we all respect her greatly as a person and as an author. She has turned up at functions full of lads and simply mingled in like a good-un.

I could go on and on and most probably have. I am Albion 100%, never doubt that and never doubt me.

Tony: I hope you enjoyed the book I'm just so delighted and honoured to put West Brom's side across as a lot that was written about us in other books didn't ring true.

Looking back over our battles, I honestly can't say there are many regrets with regards to the actual taking part and putting myself at the forefront of violent situations. All lads involved in all football firms get an unbelievable buzz and sense of notoriety being within a firm and this tribal feeling is hard to shake. Some of us become more addicted than others and so it takes over your life and things that should be a priority sadly come second to the drug that is football violence. This is where the regrets do become apparent for me. One of my biggest is my mom not being alive to see me kick the habit for good. I'm sure if she is up there looking over me, she'd approve of my part in putting this book together and is happy now I've become the proper father and husband I should have been a long time ago. My youngest, Millie, seems to have inherited my passion for the Albion and I take great pride in taking her to home games. That is the best buzz ever. The football violence days were great times in my life but now there are greater days that I cherish with my kids, Scott, Terri and Millie and my wife Vanessa.

As I write this, my mind drifts toward the youth that are active up there now. God help them! It's a different ball game now, constant filming, Section 60s, the stop, film and search tactics and dawn raids which are becoming commonplace. You have to ask if it's all worth it? Only they can answer that but my advice to them is simple. If you've got kids, get out of it now.

Some might think all this has been put together to portray me as some kind of hard-man. Me - a hard-man? No definitely not. I was just a game lad who loved fighting at matches, would never leave his pals' side and all that goes with belonging to a firm, a very game but underrated firm at that. On the gratitude side of things, well, so much to say but the biggest thank you has to go to my mom and dad who chose me that April morning back in 1965 and then bought me back to the navy blue and white half of the Black Country. Without that happening none of this would have been possible...Thank you.

Thanks for the memories...JL, Peachy, Clem, Eamon and Johnny Payne, Frankie Francis, Wingnut, Hughsy, One Punch, Guesty, Nick Shaw and all the Dudley Section 5.

Newcombe, Chrissy Lewis, the Smethwick boys Marshell, Kenton, Vince Perry, Ruddy and Gladstone. All the old Smethwick boys including, Bowie, Leftie, Crogey, Cosmic, Jumper, Pat from Buzzard, Psycho, Micky Seery and Mickey Rodgers, Mac and Budgie.

Chinda, Kulla, Harvey, Conner, Carl, Cleary, Amoss. Swag and Will from Reading. All the Whiteheath lads, especially Big Boris (RIP) and all the Scott Arms mob - whatever team they fight for.

Botfield, Leggy, Jonah, Shep, Big Alfie, Joseph and Matty Clarke, Marcus and Tony Daley. My Arsenal pals Twinny and Spencer Richards and all the Blackheath especially Mart and Steve Shaw.

All of the Nuneaton firm including Tony White, Jamie and Duggy. My great friend Malcolm Melvin and his brother Rob (RIP).

Cola, Amber, Nick, Pacey, Frizz and all the Yew Tree crew. Mutley, Harry and Lewis, the Tipton Albion, the Leak brothers, all the Clubhouse Sooty, Dave Round, Jon the Con, Malek.

The Oldbury Albion, especially me old mate Daz Guy, Steve Guy, all the Cradley lads Big Joe, Basha, Tiger, Moley, Jay. Sharkey, Danksey, Gav Wardy, Andy Price and Big Jam of Wombourne.

Tividale Albion Criddle, Badda, Wilf, Mart Roberts, Easty and Carl, Perky. Also, a special thank you to my brother, Gary, for always sticking with me through thick and thin. RIP Heath, Ronnie Bennett and Craig Fryer.

All of us must remember this....**WE ARE ALL SONS OF ALBION**.

Best of British
Freethy

R.I.P.
LEWIS BARGERFIELD.
FOREVER. FOLLOWING's V's
NEVER FORGOTTEN

ANDREW DAVID BAYLEY
'BOZ'

Special thanks to Busby's – Harvey's Sports
Bar, West Bromwich town centre